Prodigals
and Those Who Love Them

Prodigals
and Those Who Love Them

Ruth Bell Graham

Foreword by
Gigi Graham

This **Billy Graham Library Selection** special edition is
published by the Billy Graham Evangelistic Association
with permission from Baker Publishing Group.

Baker Books
A Division of Baker Book House Co
Grand Rapids, Michigan 49516

Published by the Billy Graham Evangelistic Association with permission from Baker Publishing Group. **A Billy Graham Library Selection** designates materials that are appropriate to a well-rounded collection of quality Christian literature, including both classic and contemporary reading and reference materials.

Published by Baker Books
a division of Baker Book House Company
P.O. Box 6287, Grand Rapids, MI 49516-6287

Printed in the United States of America

Library of Congress Cataloging-in-Publication Data

Graham, Ruth Bell.
    Prodigals and those who love them / Ruth Bell Graham.
       p.   cm.
    Includes bibliographical references.
    ISBN 1-59328-020-3
    Previous ISBN 0-8010-5897-X (pbk.)
    1. Christian life. 2. Family—Religious life. 3. Prodigal son (parable) I. Title.

Unless otherwise indicated, Scripture is from the King James Version of the Bible.

Scripture marked AMPLIFIED is from the Amplified ® New Testament. Copyright © 1954, 1958, 1987 by the Lockman Foundation. Used by permission.

Scripture marked NIV is from the HOLY BIBLE, NEW INTERNATIONAL VERSION®. NIV®. Copyright 1973, 1978, 1984 by International Bible Society. Used by permission of Zondervan Publishing House. All rights reserved.

Scripture marked PHILLIPS is from *The New Testament in Modern English,* copyright 1958, 1960, 1972, by J. B. Phillips.

Scripture marked RSV is from the Revised Standard Version of the Bible, copyright 1946, 1952, 1971 by the Division of Christian Education of the National Council of the Churches of Christ in the USA. Used by permission.

The Prodigal and *In Pastures Green* by F. W. Boreham are reprinted by permission of the publisher.

"Confirm, O Lord, That Work of Thine" is from *Thou Givest ... They Gather* by Amy Carmichael, copyright 1958 Dohnavur Fellowship (Fort Washington, Penn. Christian Literature Crusade). Used by permission.

"Love Knows What to Do" is from *Toward Jerusalem* by Amy Carmichael, copyright 1936 Dohnavur Fellowship (Fort Washington, Penn. Christian Literature Crusade; London: S.P.C.K.). Used by permission.

"Give Me to Hold Me Firmly to My Trust" is from *Though the Mountains Shake* by Amy Carmichael, copyright 1943 Dohnavur Fellowship. Used by permission.

Home is that place from which,
when a man has departed,
he is a wanderer until he returns.

Sir William Blackstone

You wake up every morning
not from a nightmare, but to one.

a prodigal's mother

Contents

Foreword

Understanding Prodigals

It was a warm, balmy, North Florida evening. The waves gently lapped the white sand beach outside of our hotel room, and the palm fronds rustled against the window as we dressed for dinner.

Mother was to be interviewed at an event honoring a prestigious medical institution. During the interview she answered questions about her childhood in China, her high school years in North Korea, and then her marriage to and her life with my daddy, Billy Graham. She went on to discuss her years as a mother, her joys as well as her difficulties. Those difficulties included the many occasions of making tough decisions alone, because Daddy was away preaching. She also shared about the trying years when she had to deal with her prodigals.

After dinner, many came up to speak and to thank her for her honest, open sharing. I noticed one distinguished, well-dressed woman who hung back, waiting for a chance to speak. Tension was evident and she struggled to hold back the tears. When the crowd cleared, she approached mother timidly, hesitantly.

"My son died of an overdose of drugs," she said with difficulty. "Do you think I will see him again in heaven?"

Mother, although not knowing any of the details, saw before her a mother with a very heavy heart. She answered, "If you heard a timid knock on your door one day, and you answered the knock only to find your child standing there, bruised, wounded, bleeding, dirty, and tattered, what would you do? Slam the door in his face? Or would you throw open the door and welcome him into your arms?"

Suddenly, this mother's face registered relief. I saw the load lift from her shoulders as the tears flowed down her cheeks, because she knew she was hearing from a mother who knew what it was like to have a prodigal. They hugged each other, and the woman turned and disappeared into the crowd.

Mother does know about prodigals, and this book reflects her search for God's comfort during those times in her life when her prodigals were running away from her love and care and only God could look out for them.

These stories and readings have been a great source of help to me—her daughter—who has also had to deal with a prodigal.

May you receive comfort, strength, courage, and hope as you read these pages lovingly written for you . . . for us.

Gigi

Introduction

Prodigals are as new as tomorrow's headlines, as old as the Garden of Eden. For some reason they are usually thought of as teenage boys. But prodigals are not limited in gender, race, age, or color.

They do have one thing in common: They have left home . . . and they are missed.

For any who might be waiting the return of a loved prodigal, I venture to share some of the comfort and assurance I gathered from a variety of sources during the years of our waiting.

Stories of other prodigals, some famous, some not, who returned to the Father, were a great encouragement to me. Verses from the Bible, especially on God's sovereignty, reassured me. Ultimately He is in control. And what strength is to be found in the grand old hymns!

I have also included poems I wrote, through which I struggled to express my feelings at the time.

All of these helped me. But of the greatest help were the promises of God. As John Bunyan said, "If you want encouragement, entertain the promises."

I hope, here and there, you may find in this collection something written just for you.

Storms

The rumble of thunder was only a distant threat. But the wind in the firs beside the stream, and the oaks and the pines between the bedroom window and the street, announced the storm was on its way.

All my life I have loved storms. But then, I have only experienced them from the shelter of a solidly built house, and as a child, with the warm conviction that with Mother and Daddy near, nothing really bad could happen.

The wind rose menacingly, and there was a sudden crack of thunder directly overhead. Soon I heard the patter of little feet and sensed a small presence in the room. I heard a whispered "Mom?" That was all.

The covers were thrown back in comforting welcome as one or more small, night-clad forms would slip in (depending on the severity of the storm). There, lovingly encircled, we snuggled safely together under the covers, listening to the storm, unafraid. As nature once more grew quiet, we drifted off to sleep.

It was later, when I knew they were all enduring their own individual storms, that I lay awake wishing I could share them.

At night, it was as if I could hear a whispered "Mom?" Only there was no one there. I sensed the distant thunder, and all I could do was pray.

The Prodigal Son

And [H]e [Jesus] said, A certain man had two sons: And the younger of them said to his father, Father, give me the portion of goods that falleth to me. And he divided unto them his living.

And not many days after the younger son gathered all together, and took his journey into a far country, and there wasted his substance with riotous living. And when he had spent all, there arose a mighty famine in that land; and he began to be in want. And he went and joined himself to a citizen of that country; and he sent him into his fields to feed swine. And he would fain have filled his belly with the husks that the swine did eat: and no man gave unto him.

And when he came to himself, he said, How many hired servants of my father's have bread enough and to spare, and I perish with hunger! I will arise and go to my father, and will say unto him, Father, I have sinned against heaven, and before thee, and am no more worthy to be called thy son: make me as one of thy hired servants.

And he arose, and came to his father. But when he was yet a great way off, his father saw him, and had compassion, and ran, and fell on his neck, and kissed him.

And the son said unto him, Father, I have sinned against heaven, and in thy sight, and am no more worthy to be called thy son.

But the father said to his servants, Bring forth the best robe, and put it on him; and put a ring on his hand, and shoes on his feet: and bring hither the fatted calf, and kill it; and let us eat, and be merry: For this my son was dead, and is alive again; he was lost, and is found. And they began to be merry.

Now his elder son was in the field: and as he came and drew nigh to the house, he heard music and dancing. And he called one of the servants, and asked what these things meant.

And he said unto him, Thy brother is come; and thy father hath killed the fatted calf, because he hath received him safe and sound.

And he was angry, and would not go in: therefore came his father out, and entreated him.

And he answering said to his father, Lo, these many years do I serve thee, neither transgressed I at any time thy commandment: and yet thou never gavest me a kid, that I might make merry with my friends: but as soon as this thy son was come, which hath devoured thy living with harlots, thou hast killed for him the fatted calf.

And he said unto him, Son, thou art ever with me, and all that I have is thine. It was meet [fitting] that we should make merry, and be glad: for this thy brother was dead, and is alive again; and was lost, and is found.

Luke 15:11–32

God Gave His Children Freedom of Choice

"Dad, I'm not at all sure I can follow you any longer in your simple Christian faith," stated the clergyman's son when he returned from the university for the holidays with a fledgling scholar's assured arrogance.

The father's black eyes skewered his young son, who was "lost," as C. S. Lewis put it, "in the invincible ignorance of his intellect."

"Son," the father said, "this is your freedom. *Your terrible freedom.*"

Told at our supper table by a friend

Aurelius Augustine

Hast thou not seen how thy desires e'er have
been granted in what He ordaineth?

Joachim Neander, 1680

Few men are so great that the main course of
history is different just because they lived,
thought, and spoke. Saint Augustine is one of
those few.

This fact we owe, humanly speaking, to his godly mother's stubborn love. St. Augustine, great man that he was, never challenged me personally as much as his mother, Monica. Her love, underscored by her godliness, followed him (literally) as he wandered undeterred. She "stormed heaven's gate in his behalf." I found her a refreshing source of encouragement and inspiration.

Augustine is a great "bridge personality" of history. Christopher Dawson has written of him in *St. Augustine and His Age*, "He was to a far greater degree than any emperor or barbarian warlord, a maker of history and builder of the bridge which was to lead from the old world to the new."[1]

In a little room off the King's Library in the British Museum a small exhibit is devoted to Augustine, who lived from A.D. 354 to 430. The exhibit consists chiefly of specimens of his writings, with copies of works that range from the Dark Ages to the first scholarly edition in the seventeenth century. The display gives some indication of his extraordinary popularity throughout the age of faith.

Augustine's works were more widely read than any other author's from the eighth through the twelfth centuries, and even during the late Middle Ages he was constantly being rediscovered by clever men.

He speaks to this present age as mightily and sweetly as he spoke to the age of dying Roman Imperialism because "hearts speak to hearts," and if ever there was a great heart to speak, it was his, and if ever there were small and frightened hearts who need his words, they are ours.

But Augustine's early life gave no indication he was to become such a strong voice of faith. He was born in Tagaste, a small town in what is known today as Algeria, but during his teenage years his family moved to Carthage in the part of North Africa that belonged to Rome.

A Mother's Devotion

Augustine's devout mother, Monica, taught her young son carefully and prayerfully. His brilliance concerned her deeply, especially when, as a young man, he cast off his simple faith in Christ for current heresies and a life given over to immorality.

Later, Augustine wrote:

> I could not distinguish between the clear shining of affection and the darkness of lust. . . . I could not keep within the kingdom of light, where friendship binds soul to soul. . . . And so I polluted the brook of friendship with the sewage of lust.[2]

The details of his sin may differ from ours. He had a mistress for many years and an illegitimate son. But Augustine's story is still the story of many of us:

> The loss of faith always occurs when the senses first awaken. At this critical moment, when nature claims us for her service, the consciousness of spiritual things is, in most cases, either eclipsed or totally destroyed. It is not reason which turns the young man from God; it is the flesh. Skepticism but provides him with the excuses for the new life he is leading.[3]

The Vulgar Revels of Wild Youth

Thus started, Augustine was not able to pull up halfway on the road of pleasure; he never did anything by halves. In the vulgar revels of a wild youth, he wanted again to be best, to be first, just as he was at school. He stirred up his companions and drew them after him. They in their turn drew him.

Still his mother prayed, though, as Augustine recalls, it showed no result.

> I will now call to mind my past fondness, and the carnal corruptions of my soul; not because I love them, but that I may love You, O my God. For the love of Your love I do it; reviewing my most wicked ways in the very bitterness of my remembrance, that You may grow sweet unto me (Your sweetness never failing, Your blissful and assured sweetness); and gathering me again out of my excess, wherein I was torn piecemeal, while turned from You, the One Good, I lost myself among a multiplicity of

things. . . . I was grown deaf by the clanking of the chain of my mortality, the punishment of the pride of my soul, and I strayed further from You, and You left me alone, and I was tossed about, and wasted, and dissipated, and I boiled over in my fornications, and You held Your peace, O Thou my tardy joy! . . . I went to Carthage, where shameful loves bubbled around me like a boiling oil.[4]

Carthage made a strong impression on Augustine. For a young man to go from little Tagaste to Carthage was about the same as one of our youths going from the small community of Montreat, North Carolina, to Los Angeles. In fact, Carthage was one of the five great capitals of the Roman Empire.

A seaport capital of the whole western Mediterranean, Carthage consisted of large new streets, villas, temples, palaces, docks, and a variously dressed cosmopolitan population. It astonished and delighted the schoolboy from Tagaste. Whatever local marks were left about him, or signs of the rube, they were brushed off in Carthage.

Caught in a Cult

Here Augustine remained from his seventeenth to his twenty-eighth year. He absorbed all Carthage had to offer, including the teachings of the Manichaeans (a religious sect from Persia).

Augustine recalled those dark days and his mother's continued intercession on his behalf:

Almost nine years passed, in which I wallowed in the mire of that deep pit, and the darkness of falsehood [Manichaeism]. . . . All which time that chaste, godly and sober widow . . . ceased not at all hours of her devotions to bewail my case unto You. And her prayers entered into Your presence; and yet You suffered [allowed] me to be yet involved and reinvolved in that darkness.[5]

He also recalled how God comforted his mother during that time, showing her that all things would eventually work together for good. First He gave her a vision.

She saw herself standing on a certain wooden rule, and a shining youth coming towards her, cheerful and smiling upon her. . . . He having . . . enquired of her the causes of her grief and daily tears, and she answering that she was bewailing my perdition, he bade her rest contented, and told her to look and observe, "That where she was, there was I also." And when she looked, she saw me standing by her in the same rule.[6]

Desperate over his Manichaean heresy, Monica begged a bishop, a man deeply read in the Scriptures, to speak with her son and refute his errors. But Augustine's reputation as an orator and dialectician was so great that the holy man dared not try to compete with such a vigorous jouster.

He answered the mother wisely that a mind so subtle and acute could not long continue in such adroit but deceptive reasoning. And he offered his own example, for he, too, had been a Manichaean.

But Monica pressed him with entreaties and tears. At last, the bishop, annoyed by her persistence and moved by her tears, answered with a roughness mingled with kindness and compassion, "Go, go! Leave me alone. Live on as you are living. It is not possible that the son of such tears should be lost."

Fleeing to Rome

In his twenty-ninth year, Augustine longed to go to Rome, the most magnificent city in the world, the seat of learning and, to many, the center of the universe.

Fearing for the spiritual and moral well-being of her son, Monica pled unceasingly with him not to go. But the day came that she watched with apprehension the tall masts of the ship in the harbor as they swayed gently above the rooftops. She had waited all day with Augustine in the debilitating heat for the right tide and wind for him to sail to Rome.

Augustine persuaded his mother to seek a little rest in the coolness of a nearby chapel. Exhausted, she promptly fell asleep. At dawn she awoke and searched the rooftops for the masts of the ship. It was gone.

But Augustine's heart was heavy, heavier than the air weighted by the heat and sea-damp—heavy from the lie and the cruelty he had just committed. He envisioned his mother awakening and her sorrow. His conscience was troubled, overcome by remorse and forebodings. He later wrote:

> I lied to my mother, and such a mother, and escaped. . . . That night I privily departed, but she was not behind in weeping and prayer. And what, O Lord, was she with so many tears asking of You, but that You would not permit me to sail? But You, in the depth of Your counsels and hearing the main point of her desire, [regarded] not what she then asked, that You [might] make me what she ever asked.[7]

Starting the Road Back Home

Augustine was guided to Rome and then farther north where, after listening to Saint Ambrose, bishop of Milan and the most eminent churchman of the day, he left the Manichaeans forever and began again to study the Christian faith.

One day, under deep conviction,

> I cast myself down I know not how, under a certain fig-tree, giving full vent to my tears; and the floods of mine eyes gushed out an "acceptable sacrifice to You." And, not indeed in these words, yet to this purpose, spake I much unto You: "and You, O Lord, how long? how long, Lord, [will] You be angry, for ever? Remember not our former iniquities," for I felt that I was held by them. I sent up these sorrowful words: How long, how long, "tomorrow, and tomorrow?" Why not now? Why not is there this hour an end to my uncleanness?
>
> So was I speaking and weeping in the most bitter contrition of my heart, when, lo! I heard from a neighboring house a voice, as of boy or girl, I know not, chanting, and oft repeating, "Take up and read; take up and read." Instantly, my countenance altered, I began to think most intently whether children were wont in any kind of play to sing such words; nor could I remember ever to have heard the like.

So checking the torrent of my tears, I arose, interpreting it to be no other than a command from God to open the book, and read the first chapter I should find. . . .

Eagerly then I returned to the place where Alypius [his friend] was sitting; for there had I laid the volume of the Apostle when I arose thence. I seized, opened, and in silence read that section on which my eyes first fell: "Not in rioting and drunkenness, not in chambering and wantonness, not in strife and envying; but put ye on the Lord Jesus Christ, and make not provision for the flesh. . . ." No further would I read; nor needed I: for instantly at the end of this sentence, by a light as it were of serenity infused into my heart, all the darkness of doubt vanished away.

Then putting my finger between, or some other mark, I shut the volume, and with a calmed countenance made it known to Alypius. And what was wrought in him, which I knew not, he thus showed me. He asked to see what I had read: I showed him; and he looked even further than I had read, and I knew not what followed. This followed, "Him that is weak in the faith, receive"; which he applied to himself, and disclosed to me. And by this admonition was he strengthened; and by a good resolution and purpose, and most corresponding to his character, wherein he did always very far differ from me, for the better, without any turbulent delay he joined me.

[Then] we go in to my mother; we tell her; she [rejoices]: we relate in order how it took place; she leaps for joy, and . . . blessed You, "Who [are] able to do [more than what] we ask or think"; for she perceived that You [had] given her more for me, than she was wont to beg by her pitiful and most sorrowful groanings.[8]

As we know, Augustine would go on to more than fulfill all his godly mother's hopes and prayers, becoming a bishop and a defender of the truth. Having come home at last, this prodigal would help build a house of faith that stands to this day. In the words of Malcolm Muggeridge: "Thanks largely to Augustine, the light of the New Testament did not go out with Rome's but remained amidst the debris of the fallen empire to light the way to another civilization, Christendom."[9]

Monica's Work on Earth Completed

As for Monica, her work on earth was done. One day, shortly after Augustine's conversion, she announced to him that she had nothing left to live for, now that she had achieved her lifelong quest of seeing him come to faith in Christ. Just nine days later, she died.

"Look, Mom!" our little son called excitedly. "Look! The clouds broke to pieces and one got lost!"

I looked out across the valley and, sure enough, the passing storm was dissipating and a little cloud had gotten lost in one of the coves.

Little did we know that the time would come years later when we were the clouds and he got lost. There were calls from school principals, headmasters, irate trachers, even the police.

Fleeing from You,
nothing he sees
of Your preceding
as he flees.

Choosing his own paths
how could he know
Your hand directs
where he shall go?

Thinking he's free
—free at last—
unaware that Your hand
holds him fast.

Waiting for darkness
to hide in night,
not knowing, with You
dark is as light.

Poor prodigal!
Seeking a "where" from "whence"
how does one escape
Omnipotence?

For Those
Who Love Them

For All Who Knew the Shelter of The Fold

For all
who knew the shelter of The Fold,
its warmth and safety
and The Shepherd's care,
and bolted;
choosing instead to fare
out into the cold,
the night;
revolted
by guardianship,
by Light;
lured
by the unknown;
eager to be out
and on their own;
freed
to water where they may,
feed
where they can,
live as they will:
till
they are cured,
let them be cold,
ill;
let them know terror;
feed
them with thistle,
weed,
and thorn;
who chose
the company of wolves,
let them taste
the companionship wolves
    give
to helpless strays;
but, oh! let them live—
wiser, though torn!
And wherever,
however, far away
they roam,
follow
and
watch
and
keep
Your stupid, wayward,
    stubborn
sheep
and someday
bring them Home!

Persistence and Patience

I was reading Psalm 139:7–12, putting a certain loved name in appropriately. Suddenly I realized this was another side of Luke 15—the parable of the lost sheep.

With such a Shepherd, that lost sheep hadn't a chance.

When our son Franklin was born, Luverne Gustavson, Bill's secretary at that time, gave him a little stuffed black lamb containing a music box which, when wound, played "Jesus Loves Me." It is on the bookshelf in my bedroom now beside a picture of our son in Israel holding in his arms a little black lamb.

Prophetic? Almost.

A comfort? Frequently.

This is one more illustration that when I am dealing with an all-powerful, all-knowing God, I, as a mere mortal, must offer my petitions not only with persistence but also with patience. Someday I'll know why.

The Lord of hosts hath sworn, saying, Surely as I have thought, so shall it come to pass; and as I have purposed, so shall it stand. . . . For the Lord of hosts hath purposed, and who shall disannul it? and [H]is hand is stretched out, and who shall turn it back?

Isaiah 14:24, 27

Confirm, O Lord, That Word of Thine

Confirm, O Lord, that word of Thine,
That heavenly word of certainty,
Thou gavest it: I made it mine,
Believed to see.

And yet I see not; he, for whom
That good word came in Thy great love,
Is wandering still, and there is room
For fear to move.

O God of Hope, what though afar
From all desire that wanderer seems
Thy promise fails not; never are
Thy comforts dreams.

Amy Carmichael

A Few Suggestions for Me as a Mother

I will—

Encourage.

Keep communications open at all times.

Permit person-to-person collect phone calls.

Let them know they are loved and welcome at home, *always*.

Permit the children to disagree with me, provided they do it respectfully. (And I find occasionally they are right and I am wrong.)

Make a clear distinction between moral and nonmoral issues.

Encourage.

"Mom," Franklin said one day. "The sanitorium at Mafraq sure does need a Land Rover."

Number one son had for several summers worked with a travel agency under tour director Roy Gustafson as tour escort. On each tour they visited the Annor Tubercular Sanitorium at Mafraq, Jordan.

At that point I wasn't sure what a Land Rover was— a form of security or a special kind of dog. I learned fast.

"The Jordanian army up and took theirs, no permission nor nothin'."

"Why?"

"There was a war going on, and they needed it. Now the hospital has no way of getting around. And being fifty miles out in the desert from Amman, that's tough."

"Where does one get a Land Rover?" I asked.

"Oh yes," he added, "it has to be fully equipped for the desert. In London, I guess," answering my question.

"Okay. I'll talk to Dad about it."

After Bill got home and understood the situation, he agreed something had to be done. And true to form, he wasted no time.

Jean Wilson, who had worked with us in England for years, was contacted. Would she locate a Land Rover, fully equipped for the desert, and have it ready by the following Monday morning?

She would. And she did.

Franklin had already convinced us he should pick it up and drive it to Jordan. We felt, at this point, the experience would do more for him than a semester at college, in which he was less than interested. But for obvious reasons he needed an able companion. We thought of Bill Cristobal, his college roommate.

Bill had become a Christian after he was grown. He had had three tours of duty in Vietnam as a helicopter pilot, spending his R & R's visiting and helping out missionaries in Southeast Asia. Bill is solid, sensible, loving the Lord his God with all his "heart, soul, mind and strength," and his neighbor as himself. Bill is not only a highly qualified helicopter pilot and a committed Christian, he radiates a quiet confidence and joy in life that explodes frequently into contagious laughter.

Later he volunteered to fly for Wycliffe Bible Translators, but before he would accept his first assignment, he took time off to build his aging mother an adequate comfortable house, using his Vietnam savings. That's Bill.

So we asked Bill if he would consider dropping out of school one semester and going with Franklin on this trip. He agreed.

Bill knew Franklin. He knew he was a spiritual goof-off, but the two liked and enjoyed one another, and Franklin had great respect for Bill's character as well as his ability.

As I thought of Franklin and Bill Cristobal picking up the Land Rover in London that Monday evening, driving it on the left-hand side of the road till they arrived at Dover, then driving it across France, Switzerland, Austria, Yugoslavia, Greece, Turkey, Syria, Lebanon, back into Syria, and down into Jordan, this mother's heart sank.

Unable to concentrate, I finally got my Bible and turned to John 17, our Lord's prayer for His disciples before His crucifixion. I needed to pray for our son and his buddy—somehow I felt this prayer would fit.

Suddenly verse 19 brought me up short. "For their sakes," Jesus prayed, "I sanctify [set apart, commit, consecrate] myself, that they also might be sanctified through the truth."

This was our Lord Himself praying.

I could not miss it. I could not bypass it. I had to handle it head-on.

For Franklin and his friend Bill Cristobal's sake, I needed to recommit my life to God before I could ask that He do that for them. (Bill is now a missionary in Papua New Guinea.)

I prayed, "Lord, You take care of them. I need to settle some things in my own life with You."

It is unrealistic to ask the Lord to do in someone else's life that which we are unwilling for Him to do in ours.

So, putting Bill and Franklin "on hold," I settled some things with God that day.

The load lifted, and peace came.

The Land Rover eventually and eventfully delivered to Mafraq, Franklin and Bill stayed on to help wherever they could, mainly in construction. Franklin slept on the rooftop at night, beneath the stars brilliant in the desert sky. In bad weather, he moved to the garage with a fellow worker—an Arab named Mohammed.

Here Mohammed patiently taught Franklin Arabic words and phrases night after night till they fell asleep.

And as he worked, he silently observed Dr. Eleanor Soltau and head nurse, Aileen Coleman.

Both women were fearless six-footers in a land run by males. Both had medical skills, no-nonsense Christian commitment, unlimited compassion, and the ability to enjoy life to the fullest. Both were equally unaware of the deep, lasting impression their lives were having on one American teenager who watched them as he worked.

And who grew up eventually to become Chairman of the Board of the Annor Tubercular Sanitorium in Mafraq, Jordan.

Listen, Lord

Listen, Lord,
a mother's praying
low and quiet:
listen, please.
Listen what her tears
are saying,
see her heart
upon its knees;
lift the load
from her bowed shoulders
till she sees
and understands,
You, Who hold
the worlds together,
hold her problems
in Your hands.

Human Frailty

A sixteenth-century reformer said of a certain man that "he had good cause, but wanted shoulders to support it."

John Trapp

That's me. I have, as wife and mother, a good cause—the best cause in the world—but I lack shoulders to support it. The job isn't too big for me. I'm not big enough for the job.

from an old journal

Since God has put His work into your weak hands, look not for long ease here: You must feel the full weight of your calling: a weak man with a strong God.

Lady Culross to John Livingston of the Scottish Covenanters

Doing My Part and Letting God Do His

It is good that a man should both hope and quietly wait for the salvation of the Lord.

Lamentations 3:26

As a mother, I must faithfully, patiently, lovingly, and happily do my part—then quietly wait for God to do His.

O, tarry thou the Lord's leisure . . .

The Anglican Prayer Book's version of Psalm 27:18

And He is so leisurely at times!

RBG

John Newton

Nobody's Hopeless

> The Lord hath [H]is way in the whirlwind and in the storm.
>
> Nahum 1:3

After 250 years, "Amazing Grace," a simple hymn, still touches people's hearts. Few know its origin, the story of the man who wrote it back in the 1700s. Few have sunk lower in sin, which just shows that nobody's hopeless.

She had only six more years to live, although she didn't know it. She was not strong. As soon as her sturdy sea captain husband disappeared from sight, she called her small son, John (born in 1725), to her, and together they studied. Though fragile in body, John Newton's mother was strong in spirit.

Like Hannah with little Samuel, she taught John thoroughly. Grounding him in the Scriptures, she taught him to love them. They memorized portions together. She taught him hymns and the catechism. John responded eagerly. Unlike other boys his age, he enjoyed studying more than playing. By the time he was four, he could read fluently.

John had a keen mind and retentive memory. By six, he was reading Virgil in Latin. Later in his life he reflected, "My mother stored my memory, which was then very retentive, with many valuable pieces, chapters, and portions of scripture, catechisms, hymns, and poems. When the Lord at length opened my eyes I found great benefit from the recollections of them."[1]

Newton's mother was eager for John to become a minister, and she started early to train him in the way he should go. No one could have guessed how her prayer would be answered.

Days before John's seventh birthday, his mother died. He later declared that "the Lord's designs were far above the views of an earthly parent; He was pleased to reserve me for an unusual proof of his patience, providence and grace."[2]

How Industriously Is Satan Served

Besides answering his mother's prayer, perhaps God was also protecting her from the grief of knowing the depth to which Newton would sink before God brought him back to Himself.

"How industriously is Satan served," John later said of himself. "I was formally one of his active undertemptors and had my influence been equal to my wishes I would have carried all the human race with me. A common drunkard to a profligate is a petty sinner to what I was. I had the ambition of a Ceasar [sic] or a [sic] Alexander. I wanted to rank in wickedness among the foremost of the human race. O to Grace how great a debtor."[3]

After his mother's death, Newton had an unsettled childhood and turbulent youth. He took to the sea and was forced to join the Royal Navy. Attempting to escape, he wound up in West Africa and eventually became "the slave of a black woman who lived as wife to a disreputable white slave trader named Clow. She humiliated him, and he lived hungry and destitute for two years. When he escaped that particular bondage, he returned to slave-trading and continued his life of sin. In his own words, he was an infidel and a libertine, unrestrained by convention or morality. He saw himself as a free thinker and actively tempted others into his way of life.

Notorious for the terrible oaths he used, he outswore even hardened seamen. He said, later in his years, "My whole life, when awake, was a course of most horrid impiety and profaneness. I know not that I have ever met so daring a blasphemer: not content with common oaths and imprecations, I daily invented new ones."[4]

A Jonah on Board

On one particular ship, the captain would often tell Newton, "to his great grief, he had a Jonah on board; that a curse attended Newton wherever he went; and that the troubles met with in the voyage, were owing to his having taken Newton into the vessel."[5]

One day in a violent storm, it seemed as though the ship were sinking and everything would be lost. Newton suddenly exclaimed, "If nothing could be done the Lord have mercy upon us."[6]

He went back to his cabin and thought about what he had just said and what it meant. He had thought he didn't believe in God at all, but somehow he realized there, in the middle of the storm, he knew there was a God. And after that, his life gradually changed.

Later Newton wrote, "I, who was a willing slave of every evil, possessed with a legion of unclean spirits, have been spared, and saved, and changed, to stand as a monument of [God's] almighty power for ever."[7]

Newton continued in slave-trading even after being converted. At that time it was looked upon as a respectable business. But he became increasingly uncomfortable with it, although he attempted to be kind to those he carried in chains. In 1755 he gave up the sea, and for nine years, he worked with the custom house in Liverpool. After some time had passed, Newton entered the Anglican ministry.

Amazing Grace

Newton preached that God is love. "But the phrase can have no meaning to those who are not aware of sin," he said, often adding, "I am one of the most astonishing instances of the mercy and forbearance of God upon the face of the earth."

In addition to regular church services, he led a weekly prayer meeting. At this prayer meeting he persuaded his friend William Cowper, who later became famous as a poet, to write hymns for the occasion. So they took turns writing a new hymn for each weekly meeting.

The *Olney Hymns*, a collection of these new hymns, was reprinted year after year in America as well as in England, and thousands of copies were sold. The best are found in most modern hymnbooks (including some in translations), and it is no exaggeration to say that through these hymns Newton and Cowper still maintain a considerable spiritual influence in the world. "Amazing Grace," written by Newton, comes from that collection.

> Amazing grace, how sweet the sound,
> That saved a wretch like me!
> I once was lost but now am found,
> Was blind but now I see.
>
> 'Twas grace that taught my heart to fear,
> And grace my fears relieved;
> How precious did that grace appear
> The hour I first believed!
>
> Thru many dangers, toils and snares
> I have already come;
> 'Tis grace hath brought me safe thus far,
> And grace will lead me home.

And when this flesh and heart shall fail,
And mortal life shall cease,
I shall possess within the veil
A life of joy and peace.

When we've been there ten thousand years,
Bright shining as the sun,
We've no less days to sing God's praise
Than when we'd first begun.[8]

Jessye Norman, interviewed by Bill Moyers, suggested the tune might well have been originally from the very slaves he brought to America. When you listen carefully, it sounds almost as if it had been wrung from the hearts of the slaves in their suffering.

Of his slave-trading days, Newton said he hoped it would "always be a subject of humiliating reflection [that he] was once an active instrument in a business in which [his] heart now shudders."

Toward the end of 1779, Newton was offered the pulpit of Saint Mary Wollnoth in the city of London.

How Newton Met Wilberforce

At twenty-six years old, William Wilberforce was already a distinguished statesman. Everyone knew him as a member of Parliament and a close friend of the prime minister, William Pitt. A member of five exclusive clubs, Wilberforce also had a special musical talent. The Prince of Wales had been heard to say he would go to any party where there was a chance Wilberforce might sing. But despite this young man's personal and professional rise, he had a deep spiritual hunger.

Newton had recently completed a series of lectures on *The Pilgrim's Progress,* and Wilberforce sought him out for spiritual counsel. A time was set for them to meet, but when Wilberforce arrived near Newton's house, he walked round and round, hesitating. Wilberforce wanted his approach to Newton kept secret, because it would have been disreputable for someone of his social standing to be seen with "religious zealots." Despite his fears, however, Wilberforce eventually went in and met with Newton, and the two became close friends.

Wilberforce said he never spent a half hour in Newton's company without hearing some allusion to slavery and Newton's remorse for his early share in the trade. This knowledge of what he had been was always with Newton and was the source of his power in preaching God's grace—for he had tasted it himself.

Newton encouraged Wilberforce to remain in Parliament. For much of the forty-five years he served, Wilberforce pressed for the abolition of slavery. Near the end of Newton's life, Wilberforce (together with celebrated historian John Fox) successfully moved Parliament to outlaw slave trade in England.

When Newton heard the legislation had passed, he wrote to Wilberforce, "Though I can scarcely see the paper before me I must attempt to express my thankfulness to the Lord, and to offer my congratulations to you for the success which he has so far been pleased to give to your unwearied endeavors for the abolition of the slave trade. . . . Whether I who am within two months of entering my eightieth year shall live to see the accomplishment will, I trust, give me daily satisfaction so long as my declining faculties are preserved."[9]

William Jay, another minister, told the story of calling on Newton one day and hearing him say, "I am glad to see you, for I have just received a letter from Bath, and you may know something of the writer," mentioning his name.

Jay told him he knew the writer, and he was a most awful character.

"But," said Newton, "he writes now like a penitent."

"He may be such," Jay said, "but, if he be, I shall never despair of the conversion of anyone again."

"Oh," said Newton, "I never did, since God saved me."[10]

A few weeks before he died, Newton said to a visitor, "My memory is nearly gone; but I remember two things: that I am a great sinner, and that Christ is a great savior."

For Those
Who Love Them

In Evil Long I Took Delight

In evil long I took delight,
Unawed by shame or fear,
Till a new object struck my sight,
And stopped my wild career.

   I saw One hanging on a tree,
   In agonies and blood,
   Who fixed His languid eyes on me,
   As near His cross I stood.

      Sure never till my latest breath
      Can I forget that look:
      It seemed to charge me with His death,
      Though not a word He spoke.

         My conscience felt and owned the guilt,
         It plunged me in despair;
         I saw my sins His blood had spilt,
         And helped to nail Him there.

            Alas! I knew not what I did!
            But now my tears are vain:
            Where shall my trembling soul be hid?
            For I the Lord have slain!

               A second look He gave, which said,
               "I freely all forgive;
               This blood is for thy ransom paid:
               I die, that thou mayst live."

                  Thus, while His death my sin displays
                  In all its blackest hue,
                  Such is the mystery of grace,
                  It seals my pardon too.

                     With pleasing grief, and mournful joy,
                     My spirit now is filled,
                     That I should such a life destroy,
                     Yet live by Him I killed.

John Newton

I Am Your Child

"I am your child. Do you know me?
I cannot cry out as once I did
Ten years, fifteen, now past.
Then you knew, as I did,
That I needed you.

"I am your child. Can you hear me?
My cry is muffled in withdrawal.
Transformed into rebellion, bitter
unlovely, reaching out for love.
Mother! Are you there?"

Nancy S. Hornick

An Empty Bottle and a Dying Child

I, as a mother, need to walk with God in loving obedience, feeding on His promises. If I lose heart, how can I be of any help?

I was reading the sad story of Hagar and Ishmael in the desert (Gen. 21:15) where "the water was spent in the bottle."

And I read what John MacNeil wrote of the well of water springing up, as the "Spirit-filled and overflowing life." That well so often and so easily becomes spent: "'Tis a painful experience wandering in the wilderness with an empty bottle and a dying child."

Oh, God, help me!

"Help, Lord . . . " (Ps. 12:1) means, according to John Trapp (that delightful seventeenth-century Puritan), "Help! at a dead lift."

from an old journal

Immortal, Invisible, God Only Wise

Immortal, invisible, God only wise,
in light inaccessible hid from our eyes,
most blessed, most glorious, the Ancient of Days,
almighty, victorious, thy great name we praise.

Unresting, unhasting, and silent as light,
nor wanting, nor wasting, thou rulest in might;
thy justice like mountains high soaring above
thy clouds, which are fountains of goodness and love.

To all life thou givest, to both great and small;
in all life thou livest, the true life of all;
we blossom and flourish as leaves on the tree,
and wither and perish—but naught changeth thee.

Great Father of glory, pure Father of light,
thine angels adore thee, all veiling their sight;
all praise we would render; O help us to see
'tis only the splendor of light hideth thee.

Walter Chalmers Smith

For some reason, singing this old hymn has given me much reassurance.

Worship and Worry

There is no situation so chaotic that God cannot, from that situation, create something that is surpassingly good. He did it at the creation. He did it at the cross. He is doing it today.

Bishop Moule

It was early in the morning in another country. Exhausted as I was, I awoke around three o'clock. The name of someone I loved dearly flashed into my mind. It was like an electric shock.

Instantly I was wide awake. I knew there would be no more sleep for me the rest of the night. So I lay there and prayed for the one who was trying hard to run from God. When it is dark and the imagination runs wild, there are fears only a mother can understand.

Suddenly the Lord said to me, "Quit studying the problems and start studying the promises."

Now, God has never spoken to me audibly, but there is no mistaking when He speaks. So I turned on the light, got out my Bible, and the first verses that came to me were Philippians 4:6–7: "Be careful for nothing; but in every thing by prayer and supplication *with thanksgiving* let your requests be made known unto God. And the peace of God, which passeth all understanding, shall keep your hearts and minds through Christ Jesus" (italics mine).

Or, as the Amplified Version has it, "Do not fret or have any anxiety about anything, but in every circumstance and in everything by prayer and petition [definite requests] *with thanksgiving* continue to make your wants known to God" (italics mine).

Suddenly I realized the missing ingredient in my prayers had been "with thanksgiving." So I put down my Bible and spent time worshiping Him for who and what He is. This covers more territory than any one mortal can comprehend. Even contemplating what little we do know dissolves doubts, reinforces faith, and restores joy.

I began to thank God for giving me this one I loved so dearly in the first place. I even thanked Him for the difficult spots that taught me so much.

And you know what happened? It was as if someone turned on the lights in my mind and heart, and the little fears and worries that had been nibbling away in the darkness like mice and cockroaches hurriedly scuttled for cover.

That was when I learned that worship and worry cannot live in the same heart: they are mutually exclusive.

Wait

Wait for this reasonable aid
And though it tarry, wait.
The promise may be long delayed,
But cannot come too late.

William Cowper

For Our Help

For our help, we mothers have:

His precepts
His presence
His provision
His promises
His power

His precepts

Psalm 19:7–11

His presence

Among the greatest promises
of God are the "I am with
you" promises. They begin in
Genesis 26:24 and end with
Matthew 28:20.

His provision

Philippians 4:19
God—what a source
His riches in glory—what a
 supply
Christ Jesus—what a channel

His promises

2 Corinthians 1:20
"Truth and assurance," said
John Trapp in the seven-
teenth century, ". . . will eat
their way over all alps of
opposition."

His power

Romans 15:13
Saved by His power
Kept by His power
Have hope by His power

I Know He Has Answered Prayer

'Twas He who taught me thus to pray
And I know He has answered prayer,
But it has been in such a way
As almost drove me to despair.

Anonymous

Men may spurn our appeals, reject our message, oppose our arguments, despise our persons—but they are helpless against our prayers.

Sidlow Baxter

The Fear of the Lord

O that there were such an heart in them, that they would fear me, and keep all my commandments always, that it might be well with them, and with their children for ever!

Deuteronomy 5:29

From Genesis to Revelation, *fear of God and obedience to God are two key commands.*

If we fall short in either of these, our children, as well as we, will suffer.

In the fear of the Lord is strong confidence: and his children shall have a place of refuge.

Proverbs 14:26

Fear of the Lord puts all other fears in proper perspective.

3

Flora Campbell in the Scottish Glen of Drumtochty

Ian Maclaren

> They left, and we ask, "Why? . . .
> Lord, was it I!"

It seemed to the other elders that Lachlan Campbell dealt hard with the young people, especially those who had gone astray, but they learned one evening that his justice at least had no partiality.

One elder, Burnbrae, said afterward that Lachlan "looked like a ghost comin' in at the door." But Lachlan sat in silence in the shadow, and no one marked the agony on his face till the end.

A Terrible Calamity

"If that is all the business, moderator, I must bring a case of discipline before the Session, and ask them to do their duty," Lachlan began. "It is known to me that a young woman who has been a member of this church has left her home and gone into the far country. There will be no use in summoning her to appear before the Session, for she will never be seen again in this parish. I move that she be cut off from the roll, and her name is—" Lachlan's voice broke, but in an instant he recovered. "Her name is Flora Campbell."

Carmichael the minister confessed later he was stricken dumb, and that Lachlan's ashen face held him with an awful fascination. It was Burnbrae who first found a voice: "Moderator, this is a terrible calamity that has befallen our brother, and I'm feelin' as if I had lost a little one o' my own, for a sweeter lassie didna cross our kirk [church] door. None o' us want to know what has happened or where she has gone, and not a word o' this will cross our lips. Her father's done more than could be expected o' mortal man, and now we have our duty.

"It's not the way o' this Session to cut off any member o' the flock at a stroke, and we will not begin with Flora Campbell. I move, moderator, that the case be left to her father and yourself, and our neighbor may depend on it that Flora's name and his will be mentioned in our prayers, every mornin' and night till the good Shepherd o' the sheep brings her home."

Brunbrae paused and then, with tears in his voice—men do not weep in the Scottish glen of Drumtochty—added, "With the Lord there is mercy, and with Him is plenteous redemption."

The minister took the old man's arm, led him into the manse [minister's home] and set him in the big chair by the study fire.

"Thank God, Lachlan, we are friends now; tell me about it as if I were your son and Flora's brother."

Flora's Foolishness

The father took a letter from his pocket with a trembling hand:

Dear Father,

When this reaches you I will be in London and not worthy to cross your door. Do not be always angry with me, and try to forgive me, for you will not be troubled any more by my dancing or dress. Do not think that I will be blaming you, for you have been a good father to me, and said what you would be considering right, but it is not easy for a man to understand a girl. Oh, if I had my mother, then she would have understood me and I would not have crossed you.

Forget poor Flora's foolishness, but you will not forget her, and maybe you will still pray for me. Take care of the geraniums for my sake, and give milk to the lamb that you called after me. I will never see you again, in this world or the next, nor my mother. . . . [Here the letter was much blotted.] When I think that there will be no one to look after you, and have the fire burning for you on winter nights, I will be rising to come back. But it is too late, too late. Oh, the disgrace I will be bringing on you in the glen.

Your unworthy daughter,
Flora Campbell

"This is a fiery trial, Lachlan, and I cannot even imagine what you are suffering," said the minister. "But do not despair, for that is not the letter of a bad girl. Perhaps she was impatient and has been led astray. But Flora is good at heart, and you must not think she is gone forever."

Lachlan groaned, the first sound he had made, and then he tottered to his feet. "You are kind, Master Carmichael, and so was Burnbrae, and I will be thankful to you all, but you do not understand. Oh no, you do not understand."

I Have No Daughter

Lachlan caught hold of a chair and looked the minister in the face. "She has gone, and there will be no coming back. You would not take her name from the roll of the church, and I will not be meddling with that book. But I have blotted out her name from my Bible, where her mother's name is written and mine. She has wrought confusion in Israel and in an elder's house, and I . . . I have no daughter.

"But I loved her, she never knew how I loved her, for her mother would be looking at me from her eyes."

The minister walked with Lachlan to the foot of the hill on which his cottage stood. After they had shaken hands in silence, the minister watched the old man's figure in the cold moonlight till he disappeared into the forsaken home, where the fire had gone out on the hearth, and neither love nor hope was waiting for a broken heart.

The railway did not think it worthwhile to come to Drumtochty, and the glen was cut off from the lowlands by miles of forest, so manners retained the fashion of the former age. Six elders, besides the minister, knew the tragedy of Flora Campbell and never opened their lips.

Mrs. Macfadyen, who was Drumtochty's newspaper and understood her duty, refused to pry into this secret. The pity of the glen went out to Lachlan, but no one even looked a question as he sat alone in his pew or came down on a Saturday afternoon to the village shop for his week's provisions.

His Heart Is Breakin'

"It makes my heart weep to see him," Mrs. Macfadyen said one day. "So bowed an' distracted, him that was so tidy and firm. His hair's turned white in a month, and he's away to nothin' in his clothes. But least said is soonest mended. It's not right to interfere wi' another's sorrow. We must just hope that Flora'll soon come back, for if she does not, Lachlan'll no be long wi' us. He's sayin' nothin', and I respect him for it; but anybody can see his heart is breakin'."

Everyone was helpless till Marget Howe met Lachlan in the shop and read his sorrow at a glance. She went home to Whinnie Knowe in great distress.

"It was woesome to see the old man gathering his bit things wi' a shaking hand, and speaking to me about the weather, and all the time his eyes were saying, 'Flora, Flora.'

"It's laid on me to visit Lachlan, for I'm thinking our Father didna comfort us without expecting that we would comfort other fold."

When Marget came round the corner of Lachlan's cottage, she found Flora's plants laid out in the sun and her father watering them on his knees. One was ready to die.

He was taken unawares, but in a minute he was leading Marget in with hospitable words: "It's kind of you to come to an old man's house, Mistress Howe, and it's a very warm day. You will not care for spirits, but I am very good at making tea."

Marget spoke at once: "Master Campbell, you will believe that I have come in the love of God and because we have both been afflicted. I had a son, and he is gone; you had a daughter, and she is gone. I know where George is and am satisfied. I think your sorrow is deeper than mine."

"Would to God that she was lying in the kirkyard; but I will not speak of her," Lachlan answered. "She isn't anything to me this day. See, I will show you what I have done, for she has been a black shame to her name."

He opened the Bible, and there was Flora's name scored with wavering strokes, but the ink had run as if it had been mingled with tears.

You Have the Greater Shame

Marget's heart burned within her at the sight, and she could hardly make allowance for Lachlan's blood and theology. "This is what you have done, and you let a woman see your work. You are an old man, and in sore travail, but I tell you before God, you have the greater shame. Just twenty years o' age this spring, and her mother dead. No woman to watch over her, and she wandered from the fold, and all you can do is to take her out o' your Bible. Woe is me if our Father had blotted out our names from the Book o' Life when we left His house. But He sent His Son to seek us, an' a weary road He came. I tell you, a man would not leave a sheep to perish as you have cast off your own child. You're worse than Simon the Pharisee, for Mary was not kin to him. Poor Flora, to have such a father."

"Who will be telling you that I was a Pharisee?" cried Lachlan, quivering in every limb and grasping Marget's arm.

"Forgive me, Lachlan, forgive me. It was the thought o' the misguided lassie carried me, for I did not come to upbraid you."

But Lachlan had sunk into a chair and had forgotten her.

God Be Merciful to Me, a Sinner

"She has the word, and God will have smitten the pride of my heart, for it is Simon that I am," he said. "I was hard on my child, and I was hard on the minister, and there was none like me. The Lord has laid my name in the dust, and I will be angry with her. But she is the scapegoat for my sins and has gone into the desert. God be merciful to me, a sinner."

So Marget knew it would be well with Lachlan yet, and she wrote this letter:

My dear lassie,

You know that I was always your friend, and I am writing this to say that your father loves you more than ever and is wearing out his heart for the sight o' your face. Come back, or he'll die through want o' his born.

The glen is bright and bonny now, for the purple heather is on the hills, and down below the golden corn, wi' bluebell and poppy flowers between. Nobody will ask you where you've been or anything else; there's not a child in the place that's not wearying to see you; and, Flora, lassie, if there will be such gladness in our wee glen when you come home, what think you o' the joy in the Father's house? Start the very minute you get this letter; your father bids you come, and I'm writing this in place o' your mother.

Marget Howe

Marget went out to tend the flowers while Lachlan read the letter, and when he gave it back, the address was written in his own hand.

He went as far as the crest of the hill with Marget and watched her on the way to the post office till she was only a speck on the road. When he went back into his cottage, the shadows were beginning to fall, and he remembered it would soon be night.

"It is in the dark that Flora will be coming, and she must know that her father is waiting for her."

He cleaned and trimmed a lamp that was kept for show and had never been used. Then he selected from his books Edwards's *Sinners in the Hands of an Angry God,* and on it he laid the large family Bible out of which Flora's name had been blotted. This was the stand on which he set the lamp in the window, and every night its light shone down the steep path ascending to Flora's home.

The Prodigal Returns

It was only by physical force and strength of personalities that the Kildrummie passengers could get on the train at the junction, and the Drumtochty men were always the last to capitulate. They watched the main line train disappear in the distance, then broke into groups to discuss the cattle sale, while Peter Bruce, the baggage handler, drove his way through their midst with large pieces of luggage and abused the passengers by name without respect of persons:

"It's most aggravatin', Drumsheugh, that you all stand there complainin' about the prices, as if you were a poor cottage body that had sold her a cow, and us twelve minutes late. Man, get into your carriage."

"Peter's in an awful excitement tonight," Drumsheugh responded. "You would think he was a mail guard to hear him speak."

Peter escaped this winged shaft, for he had detected a woman in the remote darkness.

"Woman, what are you stragglin' about there for out o' a body's sight? I near set off without you."

Then Peter recognized her face, and his manner softened of a sudden. "Come away, lassie, come away; I didna know you at the moment, but I heard you had been visitin' in the south. The third car is terrible full with the Drumtochty lads; you will maybe be as handy in our second car."

And Flora Campbell stepped in unseen.

Between the junction and Kildrummie, Peter was accustomed to wander along the footboard, collecting tickets and identifying passengers. He was generally in fine trim on the way up and took ample revenge for the insults of the departure. But it was supposed that Peter had taken Drumsheugh's withering sarcasm to heart, for he attached himself to the second car that night and was invisible to the expectant third till the last moment.

"You've had a long journey, Miss Campbell, and you must be nearly done with tired; just you sit still till the passengers get away, and the good wife and me would be proud if you took a cup o' tea wi' us before you started home. I'll come for you as soon as I get the train emptied and my little chores finished."

Peter hurried up to his cottage in such haste that his wife came out in great alarm.

"No, there's nothin' wrong; it's the opposite way this night. You remember Flora Campbell, that left her father, and none o' the Drumtochty folk would say anything about her. Well, she's in the train, and I've asked her up to rest, and she was glad to come, poor thing. So give her a hearty welcome, woman, and the best in the house, for ours will be the first roof she'll be under on her way home."

Mary Bruce's hand sent a thrill to Flora's heart: "Now I count this real kind o' you, Miss Campbell, to come in without ceremony, and I'd be terrible pleased if you would do it any time you're travellin'. The rail is ordinarily fatiguin', and a cup o' tea will set you up." And Mary had Flora in the best chair and was loading her plate with homely dainties.

A Pledge of Human Forgiveness

No one can desire a sweeter walk than through a Scottish pine wood in late September. Many a time on market days Flora had gone singing through these woods, plucking a posy of wildflowers and finding a mirror in every pool; but now she trembled and was afraid.

The rustling of the trees in the darkness, the hooting of an owl, the awful purity of the moonlight in the glades, were to her troubled conscience omens of judgment. Had it not been for the kindness of Peter and Mary Bruce, which was a pledge of human forgiveness, there would have been no heart in her to dare that woods, and it was with a sob of relief she escaped from the shadow and looked upon the old glen once more.

Beneath her ran the little river, spanned by its quaint, old bridge; away on the right the parish kirk peeped out from a clump of trees; halfway up the glen, the village lay surrounded by patches of corn; and beyond were the moors . . . with a shepherd's cottage that had her heart.

Marget had written to Flora for her dead mother, but no one could speak with authority for her father. She knew the pride of his religion and his iron principles. If he refused her entrance, it would have been better for her to have died in London.

The Light in the Window

A turn of the path brought her within sight of the cottage, and her heart came into her mouth, for the kitchen window was ablaze with light. One moment she feared Lachlan might be ill, but in the next she understood, and in the greatness of her joy, she ran the rest of the way.

When she reached the door, her strength had departed, and she was not able to knock. But there was no need, for the dogs, who never forget nor cast off, were bidding her welcome with short, joyous yelps of delight, and she could hear her father feeling for the latch, which for once could not be found, and saying nothing but "Flora, Flora."

She had made up some kind of speech, but the only word she could now say was "Father," for Lachlan, who had never even kissed her all the days of her youth, clasped her in his arms and sobbed out blessings over her head, while the dogs licked her hands with their soft, kindly tongues.

"It is a pity you don't speak Gaelic," Flora later said to Marget. "It is the best of all languages for loving. There are fifty words for darling, and my father will be calling me every one that night I came home."

Lachlan was so carried with joy, and firelight is so hopeful, that he had not seen the signs of sore sickness on Flora's face. But the morning light undeceived him, and he was sadly dashed.

"You will be very tired after your long journey, Flora, and it is good for you to rest. There is a man in the village I am wanting to see, and he may be comin' back with me."

Let Not the Child Suffer for Her Father's Sins

Then Lachlan went to his place of prayer and lay on the ground and cried, "Have mercy on me, O Lord, and spare her for Thy servant's sake. Take her not till she has seen that I love her. Give me time to do her kindness for the past wherein I oppressed her. Turn away Thy judgment on my hardness, and let not the child suffer for her father's sins."

Then he arose and hastened for the doctor.

It was afternoon before Dr. MacLure could come, but the very sight of his face, which was as the sun in its strength, let light into the room where Lachlan sat at the bedside holding Flora's hand and making woeful pretense that she was not ill.

"Well, Flora," said the doctor, "you've got back from your visit, and I tell you we've missed you most terrible. I doubt the south country folk have been feeding you over well, or maybe it was the town air. It never agrees with me."

Flora put an arm around her father's neck and drew down his face to hers, but the doctor was looking the other way. "Don't worry about medicine," the doctor said. "Just give her plenty o' fresh milk and plenty o'air. There's no livin' for a doctor with this Drumtochty air; it has not an equal in Scotland. There's the salt o' the sea and the cooler air o' the hills and the smell o' the heather and the bloom o' many a flower in it. A puff on Drumtochty air would bring back a man from the gates o' death."

You Are Not Forgotten

When Marget came, Flora told her the history of her letter: "It was a beautiful night in London, but I will be thinkin' that there is no living person caring whether I die or live, and I was considering how I could die.

"It is often that I have been alone on the moor, and no one within miles, but I was never lonely. I would sit down beside a brook, and the trout would swim out from below a stone, and the cattle would come to drink, and the birds would be crying to each other, and the sheep would be bleating. It is a busy place, a moor, and a safe place, too, for there is not one of the animals will hurt you. No, the big highlanders will only look at you and go away to their pasture.

"But it is weary to be in London and no one to speak a kind word to you, and I will be looking at the crowd that is always passing, and I will not see one kind face, and when I looked in at the lighted windows, the people were all sitting round the table, but there was no place for me.

"Then a strange thing happened, as you will be considering. It is good to be a Highlander, for we see visions. You maybe know that a wounded deer will try to hide herself, and I crept into the shadow of a church and wept. Then the people and the noise and the houses passed away like the mist on the hill, and I was walking to the kirk with my father, and I saw you all in your places, and I heard the Psalms, and I could see through the window the green fields and the geese on the edge of the moor. And I saw my home, with the dogs before the door, and the flowers I had planted, and the lamb coming for her milk, and I heard myself singing and awoke.

"But there was singing, oh yes, and beautiful, too, for the dark church was now open. There was a service in the church, and this was the hymn: 'There is a fountain filled with blood.'

"So I went in and sat down at the door. The sermon was on the prodigal son, but there is only one word I remember: 'You are not forgotten or cast off,' the preacher said. 'You are missed.' And then he would come back to it again, and it was always 'missed, missed, missed.'

"Sometimes he would say, 'If you had a plant, and you had taken great care of it, and it was stolen, would you not miss it?' And I was thinking of my geraniums and saying yes in my heart.

"And then he would go on: 'If a shepherd was counting his sheep, and there was one short, does he not go out to the hill and seek for it?'

"And I saw my father coming back with that lamb that had lost its mother.

"My heart was melting within me, but the minister was still pleading, 'If a father had a child, and she left her home and lost herself in the wicked city, she will still be remembered in the old house, and her chair will be there.'

"And I saw my father all alone with the Bible before him, and the dogs laying their heads on his knee, but there was no Flora.

"So I slipped out into the darkness and cried 'Father,' but I could not go back, and I knew not what to do. But this was ever in my ear, 'missed,' and I was wondering if God was thinking of me.

"'Perhaps there may be a sign,' I said and went back to my room and saw the letter.

"It was not long before I was on the train, and all the night I held your letter in my hand, and when I was afraid, I read, 'Your father loves you more than ever,' and I would say, 'This is my warrant.' Oh, yes, and God was very good to me, and I did not want for friends all the way home."

Lost, Now Found

"But there is something I must be telling," said Lachlan, coming in, "and it is not easy."

He brought over the Bible and opened it to the family register where his daughter's name had been marked out. Then he laid it down before Flora and bowed his head on the bed.

"Will you ever be able to forgive your father?"

"Give me the pen, Marget." Flora wrote for a minute, but Lachlan never moved.

When he lifted his head, he read:

> FLORA CAMPBELL
> Missed April 1873
> Found September 1873

Adapted from *Beside the Bonnie Brier Bush*
by Ian Maclaren (Dodd, Mead and Company, 1895)
This book is out of print but well worth
looking for in old bookstores.

For Those
Who Love Them

One Sinner More

To prosper in sin is the greatest calamity that can befall a man this side of hell.

John Trapp, 17th century

I loved Thee late, ah, late I loved Thee, Lord,
Yet not so late but Thou dost still afford
>   The proof that Thou wilt bear, with winning art,
>   One sinner more upon Thy loving heart.

Augustine

The first link between my soul and Christ is not my goodness but my badness, not my merit but my misery, not my standing but my failing, not my riches but my need.

Charles Spurgeon

Meditate on God

When I remember [T]hee upon my bed, and meditate on [T]hee in the night watches.

Psalm 63:6

How can I meditate on God during the night if my mind draws a blank? Study the following and keep searching and feeding your heart on Him and His Word.

Job 11:7–8
Job 12 and 26
Job 38, 39, 40 and 41
Psalm 147:5
Isaiah 40 (especially verse 28)
Isaiah 43
Romans 11:33
1 John 3:20

Our vital need is for a vital faith in God—in the omnipotent God. When oppressed with staggering problems, do not consider their boundaries but rediscover the boundlessness of God.

Mrs. Charles E. Cowman

Had I Been Joseph's Mother

Had I been Joseph's mother
I'd have prayed
protection from his brothers
"God, keep him safe.
He is so young,
so different from
the others."
Mercifully,
she never knew
there would be slavery
and prison, too.

Had I been Moses' mother
I'd have wept
to keep my little son:
praying she might forget
the babe drawn from the
     water
of the Nile.
Had I not kept
him for her
nursing him the while,
was he not mine?
—and she
but Pharaoh's daughter?

Had I been Daniel's mother
I should have pled
"Give victory!
—this Babylonian horde
godless and cruel—
Don't let him be a captive
—better dead,
Almighty Lord!"

Had I been Mary,
Oh, had I been she,
I would have cried
as never mother cried,
"Anything, O God,
Anything . . .
—but crucified."

With such prayers importunate
my finite wisdom would assail
Infinite Wisdom.
God, how fortunate
Infinite Wisdom
should prevail.

Authority

The Roman centurion recognized that Christ's authority was a direct result of His submission to God's authority. Jesus said: "I do always those things that please [H]im" (John 8:29), "My meat is to do the will of [H]im that sent me" (John 4:34), and ". . . if it be possible . . . nevertheless, not as I will, but as [T]hou wilt" (Matt. 26:39; see also Luke 7:8).

The Christian parent's authority will be a direct result of, and in proportion to, his or her submission to divine authority.

This is more than a once-for-all act; it is a day-by-day, moment-by-moment attitude.

> Children . . . honor thy father and thy mother.
>
> Ephesians 6:1–2

> Fathers, don't over-correct your children or make it difficult for them to obey the commandment.
>
> Ephesians 6:4 PHILLIPS

> Fathers, do not irritate and provoke your children to anger—do not exasperate them to resentment—but rear them [tenderly] in the training and discipline and the counsel and admonition of the Lord.
>
> Ephesians 6:4 AMPLIFIED

Love Knows What to Do

> For my beloved I will not fear: Love knows what to do
> For him, for her, from year to year, as hitherto;
> Whom my heart cherishes are dear
> To Thy heart too.

Amy Carmichael

Encouragement

Exhortations should have one dominant note, and that note should be encouragement.

William Barclay on Romans 12:8

Thoughts on Raising Children

Hear, O Israel: The LORD our God, the LORD is one. Love the LORD your God with all your heart and with all your soul and with all your strength. These commandments that I give you today are to be upon your hearts. Impress them on your children. Talk about them when you sit at home and when you walk along the road, when you lie down and when you get up.

Deuteronomy 6:4–7 NIV

O God, give me serenity to accept the things I cannot change, courage to change the things I can, and wisdom to know the difference.

St. Francis of Assisi

A line from Ecclesiasticus: "He giveth little and upbraideth much." How often we mothers do just that. At least I do. Ovid said, "Be slow to punish but quick to reward."

Prayer shall be made for him continually and daily shall he be praised.

In Tenderness He Sought Me

In tenderness He sought me,
Weary and sick with sin,
And on His shoulders brought me
Back to His fold again;
While angels in His presence sang
Until the courts of heaven rang.
Oh, the love that sought me!
Oh, the blood that bought me!
Oh, the grace that brought me to the fold,
Wondrous grace that brought me to the fold!

He washed the bleeding sin-wounds,
And poured in oil and wine;
He whispered to assure me,
"I've found thee, thou art Mine":
I never heard a sweeter voice;
It made my aching heart rejoice!
Oh, the love that sought me!
Oh, the blood that bought me!
Oh, the grace that brought me to the fold,
Wondrous grace that brought me to the fold!

He pointed to the nail-prints,
For me His blood was shed;
A mocking crown, so thorny,
Was placed upon His head:
I wondered what He saw in me
To suffer such deep agony.
Oh, the love that sought me!

Oh, the blood that bought me!
Oh, the grace that brought me to the fold,
Wondrous grace that brought me to the fold!

I'm sitting in His presence,
The sunshine of His face,
While with adoring wonder
His blessing I retrace.
It seems as if eternal days
Are far too short to sound His praise.
Oh, the love that sought me!
Oh, the blood that bought me!
Oh, the grace that brought me to the fold,
Wondrous grace that brought me to the fold!

So while the hours are passing,
All now is perfect rest;
I'm waiting for the morning,
The brightest and the best,
When He will call us to His side,
To be with Him, His spotless bride.
Oh, the love that sought me!
Oh, the blood that bought me!
Oh, the grace that brought me to the fold,
Wondrous grace that brought me to the fold!

W. Spencer Walton

This hymn goes back to my early days of my childhood in China, and I have loved it ever since. If in tenderness He sought me, will He not in equal tenderness seek mine?

Leave Them in God's Hands

I will contend with him that contendeth with thee, and I will save thy children.

Isaiah 49:25b

Dying of cancer, Isabel Kuhn wrote in *In the Arena*, "The future of my loved ones after I leave them? The Lord who has been kind to me will not be less so to them."

Promises, though they be for a time seemingly delayed, cannot be finally frustrated. . . . The heart of God is not turned though His face be hid; and prayers are not flung back, though they be not instantly answered.

Timothy Cruso

Now the God of hope fill you with all joy and peace in believing, that you may abound in hope through the power of the Holy Ghost.

Romans 15:13

Faith can read love in God's heart when His face frowns.

James Renwick,
Scottish Covenanter

Glimpsing His Glory

"Let [T]hy work appear unto [T]hy servants, and [T]hy glory unto their children" (Ps. 90:16).

It's with good reason the order was this way. Work appeals to the mature—but it is so important that our children glimpse His glory. That glimpse of His glory makes the work worth it all. Even our Lord, "for the joy that was set before [H]im endured the cross, despising the shame" (Heb. 12:2).

Once people have glimpsed His glory, they will suffer the loss of all things, counting them but refuse that they might win Christ. Isaiah labored a lifetime and met a grisly death—but he saw His glory first. Ezekiel saw His glory first, also. Paul, the arch-persecutor, became the Lord's prisoner—laboring, traveling, preaching, and suffering as few others have. But he saw His glory first. Peter, James, and John also suffered for Him as few have, but they saw His glory first.

We must take care, we parents, that we speak less of the problems, the difficulties, the headaches and heartaches and backaches in this work than we do of Him and His glory. Indeed, I question the wisdom of even mentioning the former when the children are small.

God! Thou Art Love!

God! Thou art Love! I build my faith on that! . . .
I know Thee, who has kept my path, and made
Light for me in the darkness—tempering sorrow,
So that it reached me like a solemn joy;
It were too strange that I should doubt Thy love.

Robert Browning, from "Paraclesus"

The Face of the Pilot

I was flying in a small plane up to the Shenandoah Valley of Virginia. The clouds hung low and piled high.

"You couldn't pay me to get in that little plane on a day like this," my driver to the airport commented.

But I had confidence in the pilot.

As the small plane bounced and pitched its way up through the clouds, I glanced at the pilot's face. I saw no worry there, just careful attention and calm efficiency.

Once he glanced back and smiled, asking how I was doing.

"Fine!" I replied and meant it.

I'm thinking how little ones watch us from time to time just to see how we're reacting to the world news, the death of a friend, the perpetuation of some gross injustice.

Our children will reflect our reactions.

I Bring Those Whom I Love

I bring those whom I love
to You,
commit each to
Your loving care:
then carry them away again
nor leave them there:
forgetting You
Who lived to die
(and rose again!)
care more than I.

So back I come
with my heart's load,
confessing
my lack of faith
in You alone,
addressing
all I cannot understand
to You
Who do.

You know each heart,
each hidden wound,
each scar,
each one who played a part
in making those
we bring to You
the ones they are
(and dearer each to You
than us, by far),

So—
now I give them
to Your loving care,
with thankful heart,
—and leave them there.

All Went Well

Then I proclaimed a fast . . . that we might afflict [humble]
ourselves before our God, to seek of [H]im a right way for us,
and for our little ones, and for all our substance.

Ezra 8:21

"And he listened to our entreaty" (Ezra 8:23 RSV). Or as
Knox translated it, "And all went well."

God's Ultimate Gift

Do I find love so full in my nature,
    God's ultimate gift,
That I doubt His own love can com-
    pete with it? Here, the parts shift?
Here, the creature surpass the
    Creator,—the end, what began?
Would I fain in my impotent yearning
    do all for this man,
And dare doubt He alone shall not
    help him, who yet alone can?

Robert Browning, from "Saul"

Learn of Him—Matthew 11:29

It was our Lord's meekness and lowliness that made His great burden so light. . . . And it is out of His own experience that He speaks to us. "Bring but a meek heart to your burden as I did," He says to us. "Bring but the same mind to your yoke as I brought to My yoke, and see how easy it will feel," . . . Go to Him in any case, and whatever He sees it good to do with you and your burden, He will at any rate begin to give you another heart under it. He will begin to give you a meek and lowly heart. . . . It is not your burden that weighs you down. It is your proud, rebellious self-seeking, self-pleasing heart. . . . Had He dealt with you after your sins and rewarded you according to your iniquities, you would not have been here to find fault with the way He is leading you to pardon, peace and everlasting life.

Alexander Whyte

Sunk in This Gray Depression

Sunk in this gray
depression
I cannot pray.
How can I give
expression
when there're no words
to say?
This mass of vague
foreboding
of aching care,
love with its
overloading
short-circuits prayer.
Then through this fog
of tiredness,
this nothingness, I find
only a quiet knowing
that He is kind.

September 1980

The Possible and the Impossible

We mothers must take care of the possible and trust God for the impossible. We are to love, affirm, encourage, teach, listen, and care for the physical needs of the family.

We cannot convict of sin, create hunger and thirst after God, or convert. These are miracles, and miracles are not in our department.

My Part (the possible):	God's Part (the impossible):
love expressed	conviction of sin
to pray intelligently, logically, urgently without ceasing in faith	creating a hunger and thirst for righteousness
enjoy being a mother	conversion
provide a warm, happy home	bringing to the place of total commitment
minister to their physical and emotional needs as I am able	showing us ourselves as we really are (without ever discouraging us!)
	continually filling us with His Holy Spirit for our sanctification and His service

Fyodor Dostoyevski

F. W. Boreham

> You don't believe my words now, but you'll come to it of yourself. For suffering . . . is a great thing.
>
> Raskolnikoff in *Crime and Punishment*

Thirty young men, dressed in shrouds (and thus, nearly naked), were led to the scaffold. The morning was bitter, the temperature below freezing, as they were compelled to stand for half an hour while the burial service was slowly read.

Facing them stood the soldiers with their muskets. A pile of coffins was stacked suggestively in a corner of the yard. At the last moment, with the muskets actually at the shoulders of the guards, a white flag was waved, and it was announced that the czar had commuted the sentence to ten years' exile in Siberia. Several of the prisoners lost their reason under the strain; several others died shortly afterward.

Fyodor Dostoyevski passed courageously through the ordeal, but it affected his nerves; he never recalled the experience without a shudder, and he referred to it with horror in several of his books.

On Christmas Eve, 1849, he commenced the dreadful journey to Omsk and remained in Siberia "like a man buried alive, nailed down in his coffin."

A New Testament and Twenty-Five Rubles

On his arrival in that desolate region, two women slipped a New Testament into his hand and, taking advantage of a moment when the officer's back was turned, whispered to him to search it carefully at his leisure. Between the pages he found twenty-five rubles. The money was a comfort to him; but the New Testament itself proved to be infinitely more.

His daughter, Aimee, tells us in her book *Fyodor Dostoyevski: A Study* (1921) that during his exile the little New Testament was his only solace.

> He studied the precious volume from cover to cover, pondered every word; learned much of it by heart; and never forgot it. All his works are saturated with it, and it is this which gives them their power.
>
> Many of his admirers have said to me that it was a strange chance that ordained that my father should have only the gospels to read during the most important and formative years of his life. But was it a chance? Is there such a thing as chance in our lives? The work of Jesus is not finished; in each generation He chooses His disciples, beckons to them to follow Him, and gives them the same power over the human heart that He gave to the poor fishermen of Galilee.

Aimee Dostoyevski believed it was by that divine hand that the Testament was presented to her father that day. "Throughout his life," she adds, "he would never be without his old prison Testament, the faithful friend that had consoled him in the darkest hours of his life. He always took it with him on his travels and kept it in a drawer in his writing-table, within reach of his hand. He consulted it in all the important moments of his life."

Discovering the Prodigal Son

In Siberia, Dostoyevski discovered the beauty of the parable of the prodigal son. Siberia was the far country. It was there that he saw the prodigal among the husks and the swine. His companions were the lowest of the low and the vilest of the vile.

"Imagine," he said, "an old crazy wooden building that should long ago have broken up as useless. In the summer it is unbearably hot, in the winter unbearably cold. All the boards are rotten. On the ground filth lies an inch thick: every instant one is in danger of slipping. The small windows are so frozen over that even by day one can scarcely read: the ice on the panes is three inches thick. We are packed like herrings in a barrel. The atmosphere is intolerable: the prisoners stink like pigs: there are vermin by the bushel: we sleep upon bare boards."

In the midst of this disgusting and degrading scene was Dostoyevski. At first glance he was by no means an attractive figure. He was small and slender, round-shouldered and thick-necked. He was clothed in convict-motley, one pant leg black, the other gray; the colors of his coat likewise divided; his head half-shaved and bent forward in deep thought.

His face was half the face of a Russian peasant and half the face of a dejected criminal. He was shy, taciturn, rather ugly, and extremely awkward. He had a flattened nose; small, piercing eyes under eyelashes that trembled with nervousness; and a long, thick, untidy beard with fair hair. The stamp of his epilepsy was distinctly upon him. You could see all this at a glance, and the glance was not alluring.

But Nekrassov, the poet, gives us a different picture, the scene as the convicts saw it. In this picture Dostoyevski appeared almost sublime. He moved among his fellow prisoners with his New Testament in his hand, telling them its stories and reading to them its words of comfort and grace. He seemed to them a kind of prophet, gently rebuking their blasphemies and excesses, and speaking to them of poetry, of science, of God, and of the love of Christ. It was his way of pointing the prodigal to the path that leads to the Father's heart and the Father's home.

For this was the treasure he found in that New Testament. This was the beauty of the story of the prodigal son. It revealed the way to the Father.

"One sees the truth more clearly when one is unhappy," he wrote from Siberia. "And yet God gives me moments of perfect peace; in such moments I love and believe that I am loved; in such moments I have formulated my creed, wherein all is clear and holy to me. This creed is extremely simple: here it is. I believe that there is nothing lovelier, deeper, more sympathetic, more rational, more manly, and more perfect than the Savior: I say to myself with jealous love that not only is there no one else like Him, but that there could be no one."

On his bended knees, Dostoyevski blessed God for sending him into the Siberian steppes. For it was amidst those stern and awful solitudes that he, a homesick and penitent prodigal, found the road that leads to the Father's house.

The parable that had opened to him a paradise in the midst of perdition was in his thoughts through all the years that followed.

Ruin Stares Him in the Face

After his return from Siberia, he found life anything but easy. Through voluntarily taking over the debts of his dead brother, his finances had become involved. Moreover, he had fallen into the clutches of an unscrupulous publisher, for whom he had contracted to write a novel on the understanding that, if it was not finished by a certain date, all the authors' copyrights would fall into the publisher's hands.

As the date approached, the impossibility of the task became evident, and ruin stared him in the face. Somebody advised him to get a stenographer, but no stenographer could be found. There was, it is true, a girl of nineteen who knew shorthand, but lady stenographers were unknown then. And the girl doubted if her people would consent to her taking the appointment.

Dostoyevski's fame, however, removed the parents' scruples, and she set to work. On her way to the novelist's house, she told her daughter afterward, she tried to imagine what their first session would be like.

We shall work for an hour, she thought, *and then we shall talk of literature.* But Dostoyevski had been seized by an epileptic fit the night before. He was absentminded, nervous, and peremptory. He seemed quite unconscious of the charms of his young stenographer and treated her as a kind of Remington typewriter. He dictated the first chapter of his novel in a harsh voice, complained she did not write fast enough, made her read aloud what he had dictated, scolded her, and declared she had not understood him.

She was crushed and left the house determined never to return. But she thought better of it during the night and the next morning resumed her post.

Little by little, Dostoyevski became conscious that his Remington machine was not only a charming young girl but also an ardent admirer of his genius. He confided his troubles to her, and she pitied him. In her girlish dream, she had pictured him petted and pampered; instead, she saw a sick man—weary, badly fed, badly lodged, badly served—hunted down by merciless creditors and exploited by selfish relatives.

Sharing the Burden

She conceived the idea of protecting Dostoyevski, of sharing the heavy burden he had taken on his shoulders and of comforting him in his sorrows. She was not in love with this man, who was more than twenty-five years her senior, but she understood his beautiful soul and reverenced his genius.

She determined to save Dostoyevski from his publishers. Begging him to prolong the hours of dictation, she then spent the night copying out what she had taken down in the day and worked with such good will that, to the chagrin of the avaricious publisher, the novel was ready on the appointed day. And, shortly afterward, Dostoyevski married her.

And then, fifteen years afterward, Dostoyevski was dying (the funeral was on the anniversary of the wedding). "He made us come into the room," his daughter recalled, "and, taking our little hands in his, he begged my mother to read the parable of the prodigal son. He listened with his eyes closed, absorbed in his thoughts. 'My children,' he said in his feeble voice, 'never forget what you have just heard. Have absolute faith in God and never despair of His pardon. I love you dearly, but my love is nothing compared with the love of God. Even if you should be so unhappy as to commit some dreadful crime, never despair of God. You are His children; humble yourselves before Him, as before your father; implore His pardon, and He will rejoice over your repentance, as the father rejoiced over that of the prodigal son.'"

A few minutes later, Dostoyevski passed triumphantly away. "I have been present," said Aimee Dostoyevski, "at many deathbeds, but none was so radiant as that of my father. He saw without fear the end approaching."

Russia, which has witnessed so many tragic and dramatic happenings, never saw a funeral like that of Fyodor Dostoyevski. Forty thousand men followed the coffin to the grave.

"When I heard of Dostoyevski's death," said Tolstoy, "I felt that I had lost a kinsman, the closest and the dearest, and the one of whom I had most need."

Clearly, we have here a man among men; a man who stirred the hearts of thousands; a man who, through his books, still speaks to multitudes. What is the secret of his deep and widespread influence? It is rooted in the story of the prodigal son.

He Is Known by His Books

Take up any of his books, and you will catch fitful glimpses of the battered volume in which he learned of the Father's love for His most wayward children. Near the close of *The Possessed,* Stepan Trofimovitch is taken ill, and Sofya Matevyevna sits by his couch, reading. What is she reading? Two striking passages from the New Testament.

And in *Crime and Punishment* there occurs a particularly poignant scene. It describes Raskolnikoff, the conscience-stricken and self-tormented murderer, creeping at dead of night to the squalid waterside hovel in which Sonia lives. Sonia was part of the city's flotsam and jetsam. The relationship between these two was one of sympathy. Each had sinned terribly, and each had sinned for the sake of others rather than for self.

On a rickety little table in Sonia's room stands a tallow candle fixed in an improvised candlestick of twisted metal. In the course of earnest conversation, Sonia glances at a book lying on a chest of drawers. Raskolnikoff takes it down. It is a New Testament. He hands it to Sonia and begs her to read it to him.

"Sonia opens the book: her hands tremble: the words stick in her throat. Twice she tries without being able to utter a syllable." At length she succeeds. And then—"She closes the book: she seems afraid to raise her eyes on Raskolnikoff: her feverish trembling continues. The dying piece of candle dimly lights up this low-ceilinged room in which an assassin and a harlot have just read the Book of Books."

This is in the middle of the story. On the last page, when Raskolnikoff and Sonia have both been purified by suffering, Raskolnikoff is still cherishing in his prison cell the New Testament which, at his earnest request, Sonia has brought him.

There is Raskolnikoff, most prodigal of prodigal sons, and there is Sonia, most prodigal of prodigal daughters, bending together over the living page that points all prodigals to the Father's house.

The candle in Sonia's wretched room burned lower and lower, and at last sputtered out. But the candle that, in a Siberian prison, illumined Dostoyevski's soul, grew taller and taller the longer it burned.

Adapted from *The Prodigal*
by F. W. Boreham (Epworth Press, 1941)

For Those
Who Love Them

God's Feathers

His father and his mother knew not that it was of the Lord.

Judges 14:4

He shall cover thee with his feathers.

Psalm 91:4

When Ned wrote from boarding school about the bad language and certain undesirable things going on (he was fourteen and newly away from home), it dawned on me that this is what God's feathers are all about. As we abide in Him, He covers us with His feathers, and certain unclean and undesirable influences will roll off our backs like water off a duck's back.

Later—much later—I learned God had not chosen to use His feathers in this way for our son. But mercifully, He did not let me know how enthusiastically this young prodigal was entering into the life of the far country.

Years after he had returned to the Father, we were talking one day. I expressed regret over having sent him to boarding school.

"Don't worry, Mom," he reassured me. "It helps me relate to others now. God had a purpose in it."

I can see it is true in his ministry today.

Moses' Wanderings

Moses' wanderings weren't
all for naught:
Wandering, he learned the
wilderness firsthand;
and later through this
"Devastation" brought
his brethren from bondage to
the Promised Land.

We Are Told to Wait

We are told
to wait on You
but, Lord,
there is no time.
My heart implores
upon its knees
. . . hurry,
. . . please!

For J. S.,
November 13, 1976

O God, the Rock of Ages

O God, the Rock of Ages,
Who evermore has been;
What time the tempest rages,
Our dwelling place serene.
Before Thy first creation
O Lord, the same as now,
To endless generations
The everlasting Thou.

Bishop E. H. Bickersteth

Another hymn from which I drew strength.

She Waited for the Call That Never Came

She waited for the call
that never came;
searched every mail
for a letter,
or a note,
or card,
that bore his name;
and on her knees
at night,
and on her feet
all day,
she stormed Heaven's gate
in his behalf;
she pled for him
in Heaven's high court.
"Be still, and wait; and see"—
the word God gave;
then she
knew that He would
do in and for and with him,
that which she never could.
So doubts ignored
she went about her chores
with joy—
knowing, though spurned,
His word was true.
The prodigal had not returned,
but God was God,
and there was work to do.

Sovereign or Not?

How reasonable to trust ourselves [or our children] to infinite love, infinite wisdom and infinite power.

Thomas Erskine

The fool hath said in his heart, There is no God.

Psalm 14:1

This goes also for those who doubt His sovereignty. Either He is sovereign or He is not. If He is not sovereign, He is not God. Therefore, when we become so preoccupied with and dismayed by circumstances and certain people that we doubt God's ability to handle things His own way in His own time, then we, too, are fools.

Note on Psalm 14:1, July 1, 1965

The Door Stands Open

In his book *Sky Pilot,* Ralph Connor tells of a young man who wandered from a good home in Scotland to one of the ranches in the Wild West. One day, as the pilot was making his rounds and going from shack to shack, he heard someone singing Psalm 23. He made his way to the shack from whence the sound was coming and there found the young man dying. He had been brought up in a good Christian home, but now he lay dying an early death through the sins he had committed.

The pilot spoke tenderly to the lad, and then he was asked to read a letter which had come to the boy from his mother that very day. He read it, and the letter closed something like this: "And oh! Davie laddie, if ever your heart should turn homeward, remember the door stands widely open, and there is nothing but joy that you will bring to us all."

That is the distinctive message of the parable of the prodigal son. There is joy in the presence of the angels of God over one sinner who repents.

God of the Universe in Power Abiding

God of the Universe
in power abiding,
whose Son both death endured
and death defied,
returning omnipotent
as before; confiding
all—all to You,
an irrevocable trust,
I find my leaden spirit
lifted from the dust
confident that You
Who've brought them
thus far on the way,
will see them through.

May 29, 1977 and June 29, 1980

5

I Wasn't Prepared
for a Prodigal

Gigi Graham

I stood in the doorway, watching my son walk slowly down the driveway and out into the street. Then, with a heart that felt heavy as lead, I reluctantly turned away.

I forced myself to go through the motions of fixing dinner and doing the evening chores. When I finally crawled into bed, I lay awake, crying and wondering. Where was he? Had he eaten supper? Did he have a place to sleep? Could we have done things differently? Would he ever come home again?

I thought back over the past months. The ups and downs, the emotions, the harsh words, the frustrations, the disobedience, the dishonesty, the questions, the long nights . . . sitting and waiting, wondering, worrying, asking, "Why?"

Why was this son choosing to rebel against all we'd offered him? A warm, loving home, physical comfort, an education, a godly heritage. We had wanted him, prayed for him, and had been overjoyed at his arrival. He had been such a fun-loving, happy child. We called him our "sunshine."

I never expected to be awakened late at night by police officers holding large dogs on tight leashes at the front door, calls from detention centers, unsavory friends, drugs, theft, wild dress to go with even wilder behavior. Why? Our other children, although not perfect, had never caused us any serious problems.

Unable to control the tears, I thought about all the chances we had given our son. He had run away from home at sixteen. We had taken him back again and again only to have him abuse our trust and disrupt our family life. We had done all we knew to do until finally, tonight, my husband had to demand that he leave our home.

I wasn't prepared for a prodigal. I never imagined that one night I would lie in bed wondering where my son was. But, once you love, you are never free again.

In looking back, I realize that the Lord allowed these difficult years and this trying situation to teach me many things.

I had to cope with overwhelming sadness that at times almost engulfed me. I had carried this child, given birth to him, cradled him in my arms, watched over him when he was sick, fixed his meals, washed his clothes, prayed for him and with him.

After years of our giving all we had to this beloved child, he chose to disregard his training and reject his teaching.

The Need for God's Presence

One night, right after he ran away, I sat down by the little lake that is on our property, crying and praying.

The night air suddenly turned chilly. I heard my husband come up behind me. Gently placing a sweater around my shoulders, he quietly slipped away again, sensing that I needed to be alone.

Soon, the small lake began to resemble a dark foreboding pool, not unlike my feelings. The lights began to go out one by one as the other members of the family turned in for the night.

I was surrounded by darkness both inside and out. "Lord," I prayed, "No one is here but You and me, and I really need a sense of Your presence. I need to know that You are here with me, so could You please let an angel appear right over there in that pine tree?" Now, I know, as our eldest son used to say when he was little, "God can do whatever God wants," so I waited in expectation. Nothing . . . no angel, no special revelation, no real sense that the Lord was there with me. So I prayed again. "Lord, if You don't want to show me an angel, could You please just let one flick his wing at me in that pine tree?" Again I waited. Nothing, just silence and more darkness.

Finally, slowly, I pulled myself up off the bench and dragged my tired body and emotions to bed. The next morning, I awoke with a heavy heart. I got up and, like a robot, fixed breakfast for the other children and ushered them all out the door for school. When the last one left, the telephone rang. It was our pastor. "Gigi, we just heard about Tullian. We will be right there to pray with you." Again the phone. A friend said, "Gigi, we just heard about Tullian . . . we love you and we are praying." Again, the phone rang. Another friend who owns his own company called to say that he was closing his business that day and taking all of his employees down to the beach to look for Tullian. Another friend brought us a check to help pay for the expenses of searching for Tullian.

All day long the phone rang. People calling to encourage, offer prayers, practical help, a shoulder to cry on . . . whatever was needed. That night when I went to bed with a little lighter heart, I said, "Lord, thank You for revealing Yourself to me in such a special way, not through an angel, but through others." This was a great lesson the Lord taught me. That this is what the church, the body of Christ, is all about. Being there for one another . . . helping to carry each other's burdens.

But I also discovered that we have to be vulnerable enough to allow certain people to know that we are carrying a burden. We don't have to be indiscriminate, tell everyone, but we need to let a few believers know, so that they can help us, pray for us, thus making our burdens a bit more bearable.

Then Came the Guilt

During those first few months and many times afterward, I experienced stabs of guilt and searing self-doubt. Could I have brought him up differently? Had I been too strict—or not strict enough? Had I shown enough love? Had I truly gone the extra mile? Had I prayed enough? I knew I had made mistakes, but I also knew that I had done my best. Sadly, there were some Christians who made remarks or looked at me in a way that made these feelings all the more difficult. However, this taught me to be more sensitive to others going through similar experiences. We need to be approachable and available, not condemning. Showing love and concern.

At times the Lord had to gently remind me to deal with my son as He deals with His children: to keep the doors of communication always open, to accept the person, even when I could not accept his actions and conduct.

But as painful as it was, Stephan and I also realized we could not allow the behavior of this one child to consume us. At times we had to purposefully put our prodigal out of our minds. It simply wasn't fair to focus all our attention and emotional energy on him at the expense of the other members of the family.

Sometimes accomplishing this was terribly difficult. We had to ask the Lord for His wisdom and discernment in knowing how to demonstrate love to our son without approving of his behavior. The Lord reminded me that sometimes love has to be tough. Sometimes lessons are only learned the hard way. So I also had to be careful not to interfere with God's dealings in our son's life, allowing him to suffer the consequences of his choices and actions—even though my mother's heart wanted to shield him.

I also had to deal with repeated disappointment. My emotions felt as if they'd been jerked along on a carnival ride. Up. Down. High. Low. Soaring. Crashing. From time to time the situation seemed improved, the tensions less, my son's attitude different. I was encouraged, and my hopes rose—hopes that he would keep his job, go back to school, be sorry, change his ways, even come home again. But soon we would experience yet another disappointment. As the years came and went I often found myself discouraged. I rode the waves of hope only to have my emotions crashed on the rocks of disappointment till I was battered and bruised.

Although there was really nothing else I could do during this troubled time, I often found it difficult to trust the Lord. I found myself wondering why God gave this boy parents if He didn't want us to be in charge. I was tempted again and again to do God's job for Him and would try my best to do something—anything—to help God out. I would interfere, manipulate, scheme, and even attempt to control the situation. My mother's heart ached for Tullian. I wanted to protect him. But it didn't help. It only frustrated me and fragmented the family.

Following are two poems written March 7, 1989, the night Tullian left home.

I sit and wait . . . wondering.
My child is late.
And my mother's heart is worried.

All is quiet . . . all is still.
All but my anxious heart.
And as my eyes fill up and spill the tears
Upon my upturned face,
I ask,
"Lord, give me grace."

Lord, bring him back.
Please bring him back into this land again.

But while he is away
With him closely stay.
And bring peace to my troubled heart.
Let the tears that start
Each day to flow
Be turned into a prayer
Because I do not know
What to do . . .
Where to start!

Lord, please take a worried mother's heart
As an offering today
And bring my boy home to stay.

Based on Jeremiah 31:10–20

Finally I wore out. The words from an old hymn became my daily prayer: "Oh for grace to trust Him more!" In response I heard a still, small voice deep within my heart saying, "Love and patience . . . love and patience."

I didn't have a problem with the love, but I had a lot of trouble with the patience part. My own mother reminded me often that I had to pray not only with persistence but also with patience.

I finally understood that if God was going to work, I had to get out of His way. I could continue to do the possible, but I had to let God handle the impossible. The greatest lesson I had to learn was to release my white-knuckle grip and allow God to be in control of all the circumstances.

I had to accept the fact that God loved my son even more than I did. And because of this fact, I could surrender Tullian to Him.

But, this is not always easy.

In fact sometimes, God asks the seemingly impossible.

My friend Linda's son was due on her birthday, but he couldn't wait. Jason was placed in her arms on the 20th of September. This little baby was to be Linda's only child. He was her pride and joy. She and her husband raised him in a loving and godly home. Like our Lord, "Jason grew in wisdom and stature and in favor with God and man." Linda rejoiced in his first smile, laughed at his first attempts to crawl, and clapped when he took his first faltering steps. She sat beside his crib praying through his childhood illnesses, tried to hold back the tears his first day at school, cheered at football games, helped with homework, offered guidance with girlfriends, and attended with pride Jason's high school graduation ceremony.

All during these years, Jason, who had made a decision for Jesus as a young boy, grew in his faith. Jason went on to a Christian college, but something happened. During his first year, he changed. He turned away from the faith, dropped out of school, and finally joined the Marines. His mother was heart-broken and heart-burdened.

One day, she penned these words . . .

How do you know if you have truly surrendered your life, your problems, your child to God? During the rebuilding of our home after Hurricane Andrew, I often found myself alone in my car many hours of the day, driving around doing errands. On one of those days, I decided to pray for Jason all day, relinquishing my hold on him and his problems, giving him up to God. I believed God loved him even more than I could, and I obviously was not making any headway in bringing him back to his belief in God and a previously joyful Christian walk. So I felt very spiritual that morning when I prayed along these lines:

"Dear Lord, I love You and praise You for Who You are and all You have done in my life. I thank You for Jason and the precious gift he is to me knowing he is a gift from You. I realize Your love for Jason and believe that it is Your will that he come back to You and turn away from the lifestyle of sin and rebellion that is dangerous to him, painful to us and heartbreaking to You. I now lay him at the foot of the cross and trust You for his salvation, his life, and our relationship with him—all so precious to me. *I trust You for Your timing, not my own,* and give him to You now. In Jesus' name I ask this. Amen."

I turned off the ignition at the first stop feeling lighter for having given my burden to God and resting in the knowledge that He would honor that prayer, confident in my Father who cares for me, who cares for Jason, and who delights in us when we completely trust Him with all we hold precious.

A few moments later, I returned to the car and started the engine but felt uneasy, restless, and not quite as spiritual as I had when I had said that amen. "O.K., God," I said, "I obviously didn't do it right, so I will pray again. Dear Lord, I really want to give Jason to You. I do trust You with all that I have and now, with all my heart, I trust Jason to You. His life, his salvation, his walk with You. I give him to You now, and *even if he is old when he turns back to You*, I believe You will draw him; I will trust You. Amen."

Second errand over, I got back in the car again. I turned on my Scripture memory music (the series for "Anxiety") and headed for stop number three. Again, I felt a nudge by the Holy Spirit. How could I be more submissive? I had given Jason to Him, trusting Him to love him back into His arms. "Heavenly Father," I prayed, "I know You want Jason to come back. I know You love him even more than I do and long for his heart again. I trust You with his life, his soul; *even if I don't live to see his return*, I will trust You."

How sad, I thought. But it was not important that I see God's work to trust He would do it, so I rested in my confidence in God's promises to mothers who pray for their children. But I did not feel rest as I returned to the car again, third stop completed.

"God, what on earth can I be missing? Why don't I feel the release that comes with truly trusting You?"

I drove toward the tile store, wrestling with what I hoped to be the final relinquishing of the worry I lived with, completely trusting God for His will in Jason's life. I ordered tile, with half my mind on the business at hand, and returned to the car. I drove toward the apartment we were living in while the house was being rebuilt and drove into the parking garage. Once more, I bowed my head in prayer, asking the Holy Spirit to give me the words to pray. Knowing that Jason was saved as a sixteen-year-old, I still wept as this prayer came: "Dear God, even if Jason dies in his sin and does not visibly come back to You, I will trust You." Suddenly very tired, but somehow lighter, I turned off the ignition and went inside.

A few months later, my friends received a telephone call. Jason had been killed in a terrible automobile accident.

After his death, his mother found this passage in his Bible, underlined during the time several years before, when Jason was close to the Lord and was in His Word:

Luke 7:11–15: "And it came about soon afterwards, that He went to a city called Nain; and His disciples were going along with Him, accompanied by a large multitude. Now as He approached the gate of the city, behold, a dead man was being carried out, the only son of his mother, and she was a widow; and a sizable crowd from the city was with her. And when the Lord saw her, He felt compassion for her, and said to her, "Do not weep." And He came up and touched the coffin; and the bearers came to a halt. And He said, "Young man, I say to you, arise!" And the dead man sat up and began to speak. And Jesus *gave him back to his mother*" (Jason's highlighting).

In the margin, Jason had written this: "She had to give him to Jesus for him to work."

God did draw Jason to Himself, not in the way his mother had wanted or expected, but God, in His infinite grace and love, allowed her to see His work being performed in the most painful experience of our lives. In the midst of the greatest pain, the greatest peace.

God asked Linda to surrender all. And, God took Jason. She doesn't know why. She is left without answers. It has been difficult at times. She has had to work through many things. But, because of her deep faith and trust in an all-knowing, loving God, she says "that it's O.K. O.K. not to fully understand."

It has been said that "beyond the revealed purposes of God there still remains much mystery. And for this there is no answer except an attitude of worship in which we humbly acknowledge that a sovereign God cannot be required to give all the reasons for what He chooses to do."[1]

The Lord has not yet asked such a great sacrifice of me. My story has a different ending.

Several years passed. One Sunday, unknown to us, Tullian and his girlfriend came to church. At the end of the service, unexpectedly, Tullian took his girlfriend by the hand and from high in the balcony, they went forward to give their lives to Jesus Christ.

I was overwhelmed with joy—but I must admit, also a bit skeptical. I didn't want to have my hopes dashed again. I waited and watched. As the weeks turned into months, we saw this young man grow and mature into a sincere, dedicated child of God. Not long after his decision he wrote about it to a Christian friend. I asked him if I could share this excerpt:

> Things went real raw after I last saw you. My whole life went down the tubes. I really fell far from the Lord. Drugs, alcohol, sex, the whole nine yards. I dropped out of school, got kicked out of my house; things couldn't have gotten much worse.
>
> But I don't want to go on about the bad stuff. I want to tell you about what the Lord has done for me. After leading a very empty, up-and-down lifestyle, I gave the Lord total control of my life. What a change. Things I used to live for don't even matter anymore. Things I used to run away from, I'm hungry for.
>
> Isn't God good? He has been so patient with me. He never gave up on me. For the first time in my life I feel peace and contentment. I don't worry about anything. I am a totally different person.

We have since celebrated Tullian's marriage to his lovely Kim, and now with two little sons of their own, they are in seminary preparing for ministry.

Tullian's Story

Everywhere you look, people are looking for something more, something they don't already have. This is most obvious in the life of a child. "More, more, give me more" is probably the most oft stated phrase that proceeds from a child's mouth. It's especially fun watching little ones at Christmastime. They stare at the presents under the tree for weeks until they are given the much anticipated "O.K." on Christmas morning. They rip open present after present; they don't even allow themselves the pleasure of enjoying one at a time. Then, to their inevitable horror, the last present has been opened and they cry at the realization that it's over. Christmas is over! What they really want is more. The anticipation that built up for weeks prior to Christmas seemed to promise their little hearts and minds more satisfaction than Christmas presents could provide. It's been said that the loneliest moment in life is when you have just accomplished what you thought would deliver the ultimate and it has let you down. But do we really grow out of this as we get older? It's obvious that we don't. We want to be faster, stronger, skinnier, wealthier. We want more power, more freedom, more stability, more flexibility. In short, the human race is made up of people who are crying out for more!

At sixteen I too was crying out for more, perhaps louder than most. The middle of seven children born to solid Christian parents, I was raised in an atmosphere where prayer and Bible reading were encouraged and practiced. I knew who God was, and I knew that He sent His Son to die on a cross for sinners. But I wanted more. I wanted to be distinct, to be heard. After all, in such a large family attention and distinctiveness are hard to come by. So instead of "casting all of my anxiety on Him," I turned to the world. I dropped out of high school, got kicked out of my house, and began living in a manner that I thought would satisfy. I craved freedom. But it wasn't until six years later that I began to realize my so-called freedom had made me a slave. A slave to desires and habits that were quickly destroying me. I had been seeking satisfaction so vigorously, that I was unconscious of just how unsatisfied I was becoming. I was hungrier at twenty-one than I had been at sixteen. The world had lied to me. Power, pleasure, and popularity had not satisfied the way I had anticipated. I was empty, and I was lonely. So at twenty-one I did what I should have done at sixteen. I turned to God. I was broken and desperately needed fixing; who better to turn to than my own personal Creator and Designer?

I was alone at my apartment in Deerfield Beach, Florida, when I got on my knees and asked God's forgiveness. I begged Him to change me. I rededicated my life to Christ that night and made a public confession a few weeks later when I responded to an invitation given at our Sunday morning church service. Unaware of my prayer a few weeks prior, my entire family watched in thanksgiving that Sunday as I grabbed my girlfriend by the hand and walked from the balcony all the way to the front of the church.

My mom had led me to receive Christ when I was a young boy, although I don't remember. During the months that followed my prayer in the apartment, I wondered whether I had really been saved prior to my recent prayer. And for a time I really believed it was at twenty-one that I first became a Christian, not as a young boy. After all, how could a Christian possibly live the way I had lived for six years? But then I began to understand the character of God. His faithfulness and commitment to His people goes way beyond my comprehension; and I had never stopped believing in Him during my time of rebellion. In fact, I remembered times during my rebellion when I had desperately called out to God, and was overwhelmed at His closeness to me. Had I lost my assurance during my rebellious years? Absolutely! But I never lost my salvation. My salvation had been secured when I prayed as a young boy, not because of *my* faithfulness, but because of *God's*.

Needless to say, life is quite different now. Things I used to live for and found significance in don't matter anymore; and things I used to run away from, I'm hungry for.

God has not taken away my excitement; He has just changed what it is that I get excited about. For the first time in my life I am content. I feel whole and complete. God has blessed me by allowing me to marry the girl I walked to the front of the church with, and we now have two precious little boys. He has given me a hunger to reach people with His truth that transforms and has allowed my life to minister to many parents who have prodigals, and to be a testimony to His irresistible grace.

The most radical truth God has taught me is that only He can satisfy our eternal longings for pleasure and peace. We would be foolish, then, to seek satisfaction in anything or anyone other than Him, in whose "presence is fullness of joy; and at [T]hy right hand there are pleasures for evermore" (Ps. 16:11).

Yes, our prodigal returned. Gratitude fills my whole being. What a privilege it has been for me, a mother, to stand back, out of God's way, and observe His grace at work.

However, my heart breaks when I realize that not all mothers, wives, fathers, or husbands who faithfully love, pray, and wait for their prodigals to return will see the answers to their hearts' cries. At least not on this side of eternity.

Saint Augustine's mother, Monica, lived to see her prayers for her wicked son answered. And can you imagine the joy she experienced when she stepped into heaven and was shown all that her son would become and do for his Lord?

My husband, Stephan, says that patience is faith seeing the finished product. Andrew Wyeth, the American artist, once said the most irritating experience for an artist is to have his work criticized before it is finished. If you have a prodigal—a son, daughter, husband or father, a mother or wife who is wandering spiritually— be persistent in prayer, but be patient. And be encouraged! Remember, God is not finished.

We don't see the whole picture from down here. My friend Linda has to live each day the Lord gives her, in faith and trust that she will one day see her boy and that together they will rejoice in the fact that behind the scenes, God was working to make all things good. If we have been as faithful as we know how to be here on earth, it will be God's greatest joy to spend all eternity making it up to us. One day the curtain will be lifted, questions answered, and faith rewarded. God will never disappoint.

So take courage, never lose hope, and keep looking up.

Recently, I was sitting behind Tullian in church. His arm was draped around the shoulders of his young wife as together they listened to the words of the song "The Keeper" that was coming to a close. "Truly, the Lord is thy keeper . . . He does not slumber. . . . He shall preserve thy going out and thy coming in" (taken from Ps. 121). Yes, the Lord has been Tullian's keeper. I glanced at Tullian; he too was having a difficult time holding back the tears.

Gigi

Afterword

It was just five years ago that I was lying in this same bed in this same back, corner bedroom.

It was late then, around midnight. I was still awake reading.

Suddenly I noticed flashing blue lights approaching. I thought they would pass on by, but instead they turned up into my daughter's drive. I heard a knock . . . then another, and another. I went to the door and discovered two policemen asking if this was the home of Tullian. I quickly said that I would go and get his parents, who were already asleep.

I quickly retreated to my room. Although I didn't know the circumstances, Tullian was in trouble again. So I prayed while his parents talked with the police.

That was five short years ago. Tullian is now married, in seminary studying for the ministry, with two little boys of his own.

His father-in-law, 59, lies in a coma, dying. Kim, Tullian's young wife, who has only been a Christian a few years, was sitting alone by the bedside of her dying father. She was singing. Later, Tullian asked her, "Honey, what were you singing to your dad?" "I was singing 'Amazing Grace'," she replied.

And so it is—AMAZING GRACE!

RBG

For Those
Who Love Them

We Are Better for Our Failures and Our Falls

"No faith," said Arthur Christopher Benson in his book on the life of Ruskin, "can have vitality or hope which does not hold that we are somehow the better for our failures and our falls, however much they have devastated our life and influence, with whatever shame and self-reproach they may have wasted our days."

There's a Wideness in God's Mercy

There's a wideness in God's mercy,
Like the wideness of the sea;
There's a kindness in His justice,
Which is more than liberty.

There is welcome for the sinner,
And more graces for the good;
There is mercy with the Savior;
There is healing in His blood.

There is no place where earth's sorrows
Are more felt than up in heaven;
There is no place where earth's failings
Have such kindly judgment given.

There is plentiful redemption
In the blood that has been shed;
There is joy for all the members
In the sorrows of the Head.

For the love of God is broader
Than the measure of man's mind;
And the heart of the Eternal
Is most wonderfully kind.

If our love were but more simple,
We should take Him at His Word,
And our lives would be all sunshine
In the sweetness of our Lord.

F. W. Faber

An old, loved hymn.

Tell Me More

The time for training children is during their early years. By the time they reach their teens, we need for the most part to keep still and listen. By that time they know what we expect of them, but they do need a sounding board. It can be inconvenient, especially if the teenager is a night owl, or if they catch you in the middle of an interesting book. Never mind, prop yourself comfortably in bed even if you have to force your eyes open. Put the book down. Stop whatever you are doing.

You're fortunate to have a teenager who wants to talk. Be interested and listen. Don't argue. And, listen.

Prayer for the Children

Holy Father, keep through Thine own name those whom Thou hast given me. . . . I pray not that thou shouldest take them out of the world, but that Thou shouldest keep them from the evil. . . . Sanctify them through Thy truth: Thy word is truth. . . . For their sakes I sanctify myself, that they also might be sanctified through the truth. . . . Father, I will that they also, whom Thou hast given me, be with me where I am.

John 17:11–24

When we pray, remember:
1. The love of God that wants the best for us.
2. The wisdom of God that knows what is best for us.
3. The power of God that can accomplish it.

William Barclay

And when He answers prayer, never complain about how.

There Has Been Wind

There has been wind
and earthquake, too;
followed by fire;*
he stood, fear-thinned,
encased, to view
the holocaust expire.

Yet—
You were in none of these:
Your still small voice next,
—please.

*1 Kings 19:3–13

Our Failures

Colleen Evans, in her challenging book *Start Loving*, quotes a friend who had written her:

> Our failures. That's the hardest area, especially when they have affected the lives of our loved ones. As our two children step out into the adult world it is a joy to see many beautiful things in their lives. But it hurts to see areas of need and struggle that stem in part from ways we have failed them.
>
> A friend reminded me recently that even these areas are part of the "all things" which God will use to make a man and a woman who will accomplish His unique purposes.
>
> So when thoughts of my failures push their way into my consciousness, I let His total forgiveness dissolve my regrets, and go on to praise Him who accepts us just as we are and lovingly works to make us more than we are.

And from the same book, "He doesn't expect us—or our children—to be finished products now."

His Lovingkindness

Awake, my soul, to joyful lays,
And sing thy great Redeemer's praise;
He justly claims a song from me.
His lovingkindness, oh, how free!

He saw me ruined by the fall,
Yet loved me notwithstanding all;
He saved me from my lost estate,
His lovingkindness, oh, how great!

Tho' num'rous hosts of mighty foes,
Tho' earth and hell my way oppose,
He safely leads my soul along,
His lovingkindness, oh, how strong!

When trouble, like a gloomy cloud,
Has gathered thick and thundered loud,
He near my soul has always stood,
His lovingkindness, oh how good!

Samuel Medley

While attending Wheaton College, one of my roommates, Kimberly Long (Wyckoff), and I would sing "His Lovingkindness" while we walked the six blocks to campus in the morning. In the evenings when we walked home, we sang heartily, "Great Is Thy Faithfulness." The idea came to us from Psalm 92:2: "To show forth thy lovingkindness in the morning, and thy faithfulness every night."

Great Is Thy Faithfulness

"Great is Thy faithfulness," O God my Father,
There is no shadow of turning with Thee;
Thou changest not, Thy compassions, they fail not:
As Thou hast been Thou forever wilt be.

Summer and winter, and springtime and harvest,
Sun, moon and stars in their courses above,
Join with all nature in manifold witness,
To Thy great faithfulness, mercy and love.

Pardon for sin and a peace that endureth,
Thy own dear presence to cheer and to guide;
Strength for today and bright hope for tomorrow,
Blessings all mine, with ten thousand beside!

"Great is Thy faithfulness!
Great is Thy faithfulness!"
Morning by morning new mercies I see;
All I have needed Thy hand hath provided—
"Great is Thy faithfulness," Lord, unto me!

Thomas O. Chisholm

Duties Are Ours, Events Are God's

Duties are ours, events are God's. When our faith goes to meddle with events, and to hold account upon God's Providence, and beginneth to say, 'How wilt Thou do this or that?' we lose ground; we have nothing to do there; it is our part to let the Almighty exercise His own office, and steer His own helm; there is nothing left for us, but to see how we may be approved of Him, and how we roll the weight of our weak souls upon Him who is God omnipotent, and when we thus essay miscarrieth, it shall be neither our sin nor our cross.

Samuel Rutherford

It Is a Fearful Thing

It is a fearful thing to fall
into Your hands, O living God!*
Yet I must trust to You my all,
praying your staff and rod**
will comfort each in need
as well as break
the wayward leg. And yet I plead
"Deal gently with the young man
for my sake." ***

*Hebrews 10:31
**Psalm 23
***2 Samuel 18:5
August 3, 1980

Watch O'er My Flock

Like other shepherds
help me keep
watch o'er my flock by night;
mindful of each need,
each hurt, which might
lead one to stray—
each weakness
and each ill—
while others sleep
teach me to pray.
At night the wolves and leopards,
hungry and clever, prowl
in search of strays
and wounded; when they howl,
Lord, still my anxious heart
to calm delight—
for the Great Shepherd
watches with me
over my flock
by night.

January 1978

God Hears Our Sighs

Hope's hours are full of eternity.

John Trapp on Proverbs 13:12

And it came to pass in process of time, that the king of Egypt died: and the children of Israel sighed by reason of the bondage, and they cried, and their cry came up unto God by reason of the bondage.

And God heard their groaning, and God remembered [H]is covenant with Abraham, with Isaac, and with Jacob.

And God looked upon the children of Israel, and God had respect unto them.

Exodus 2:23–25

The question was raised. All the time Pharaoh was alive, the Jews labored and suffered. Why then did they sigh after his death? Rabbi Manchester Mandel answered that before Pharaoh died, even to sigh had been forbidden.

Quoted by Elie Wiesel

Yet it was forty years before God sent Moses back to lead them out of Egypt to freedom.

I prayed to the Lord day and night, month after month, year after year. Was God deaf? Is He indifferent?

No. He had His reasons.

Something to accomplish in the heart of that loved prodigal. Something to accomplish in my heart.

Prayers are answered even after we're gone.

The Godly Father and His Three Wayward Sons

A godly father prayed all his life for three wayward sons. When he was dying, strangely he died in an agony of despair and doubt of his eternal salvation. The day after the funeral the three sons were discussing their father.

"If a man so godly should die in such agony, what will it be like for us?" one asked.

As a result, all three turned to God.

Told by F. W. Boreham in *The Prodigal*

We see not yet all things put under [H]im. But we see Jesus.

Hebrews 2:8–9

Give Me to Hold Me Firmly to My Trust

My God, who has committed to my care
   Thy ransomed one
Lest I be scattered here and there
   and she be gone
Give me to hold me firmly to my trust
   Let all that would distract me be as dust.
'Thy life for hers'—O solemn, urgent word—
   Lest I forget,
My sense of values waver, or be blurred,
   Or overset
By other things, take me and purge and bend
   Each power and purpose to one single end.
Teach me to do the thing that pleaseth Thee
   O Lord, my God.
Give clearness, lest some by-way tangle me.
   Where Christ hath trod
There would I tread, nor ever turn aside,
   Lest she be missing for whom Christ hath died.

Amy Carmichael

Prayer by a Bishop for the Members of His Church
(Adapted as Prayer of a Mother for Her Children)

Jesus, good Shepherd, they are not mine but Yours,
for I am not mine but Yours.
I am Yours, Lord, and they are Yours,
because by Your wisdom You have created
both them and me,
and by Your death You have redeemed us.
So we are Yours, good Lord, we are Yours,
whom You have made with such wisdom
and bought so dearly.
Then if You commend them to me, Lord,
You do not therefore desert me or them.
You commend them to me:
I commend myself and them to You.
Yours is the flock, Lord, and Yours is the shepherd.
Be Shepherd of both Your flock and shepherd.

You have made an ignorant mother,
a blind leader, an erring ruler:
teach the mother You have established,
guide the leader You have appointed,
govern the ruler You have approved.

I beg You,
teach me what I am to teach,
lead me in the way that I am to lead,
rule me so that I may rule others.
Or rather, teach them, and me through them,
lead them, and me with them,
rule them, and me among them.

> Anselm (1033–1099), Archbishop of Canterbury,
> translated by Sister Benedicta Ward, S.L.G.
> Adapted for mothers by RBG

Moses Prays to "Go Over"

"Let me go over and see the good land beyond the Jordan—that fine hill country and Lebanon." But because of you the LORD was angry with me and would not listen to me. "That is enough," the LORD said. "Do not speak to me anymore about this matter."

Deuteronomy 3:25–26 NIV

More than two thousand years later:

Just then there appeared before them Moses and Elijah, talking with Jesus.

Matthew 17:3 NIV

God answers prayer in His own way, in His own time.

But, beloved, be not ignorant of this one thing, that one day is with the Lord as a thousand years, and a thousand years as one day.

2 Peter 3:8

I Think It Harder, Lord

I think it harder,
Lord, to cast
the cares of those I love
on You,
than to cast mine.
We, growing older,
learn at last
that You
are merciful
and true.
Not one time
have You failed me,
Lord—
why fear that You'll
fail mine?

January 1976

A P.S. of Thoughts

Lord, with My Jacob, I Would Pray

"Lord,
with my Jacob," I would pray,
"wrestle till the break of Day";
till he, knowing who Thou art,
tho' asked, will not let Thee depart;
saying, "I'll not let Thee free
saving Thou wilt first bless me."

O God of Jacob, who knew how
to change supplanters then, so now
deal, I pray, with this my son,
though he may limp when Thou art
done.

Based on Genesis 32:24–31

Some Terrible Inheritance

The free gift of grace with which God perfects our efforts may come in many ways, but I am convinced that it is the common experience of Christians that it does come. There may be some souls whose brave and bitter lot it is to conquer comfortless.

Perhaps some terrible inheritance of some strong sin from the father is visited upon the son, and, only able to keep his purpose pure, he falls as fast as he struggles up, and still struggling falls again. Soft moments of peace with God and man may never come to him. He may feel himself viler than a thousand trumpery souls who could not have borne his trials for a day.

For you and me is reserved no such cross and no such crown as theirs who falling still fights, and fighting fall, with their faces Zion-wards, into the arms of the everlasting Father. "As one whom his mother comforteth shall be the healing of their wounds."

Juliana Horatia Ewing

The Murderer

Sin always affects the innocent.

Once you have loved one prodigal, you will love all prodigals.

Mercifully, God brought ours back to Himself while we were still living. We pray they both will always be kept for Him—for His glory and His joy.

But we have others who have wandered afar. For them I claim the following:

"O LORD God of our fathers, art not [T]hou God in heaven? and rulest not [T]hou over all the kingdoms of the heathen? and in [T]hine hand is there not power and might, so that none is able to withstand [T]hee?" (2 Chron. 20:6).

There was one gentle, brilliant, sensitive soul I had known for some time. He loved the Lord.

Years later, one dark day he murdered his best friend (drugs were involved). After visiting him in prison, convinced of his deep repentance, I wrote one poem as if he were speaking. The other was my prayer for him.

Today, I don't know where he is.

The Murderer's Prayer

Beyond all custom
and tradition,
Lord, I would see
Your truth revealed;
then could I come
in my condition
to seek Your face
and, by Your grace,
be healed.

What I confess,
You long have known
—acknowledge the gross
mess
that my own sins have
grown
—and mine alone—
like some wild
poisonous vine
enmeshing other lives
with mine.

"Just as I am"
to me confirms
that none
but You would take
one
on such terms.

For only You,
who went the length
of Calvary,
could know the cost
of such forgiveness
or show
Satan and his hordes
justice
has been done.

And I
defeated by that cross
freed from his cords
kneeling,
glory in my loss
For
You have won.

And
for all
my sins have wounded
on the way
I ask Your special help
—for them I pray.

April 5, 1977

Prayer for the Murderer

I leave him in Your hands, O God
who are both merciful and just.
Numb with the horror of this deed,
its hideous stench, one surely must
know how to pray.
Yet I am still
sickened to silence.
What can one say?
Was he Your son?
If so
then You will know
what must be done.
For he will be in black despair
lest he has sinned
beyond all mercy—
all repair.
What he has done,
is done. No prayer—
no penance—nothing—
can undo the loathsome deed.
yet he
is Yours.
And I would plead,
Lord, let him see
long and stark and clear
Your Calvary.

May 31, 1976

The Wildwood Is Worse for the Wanderer

The man who yields to the world, the flesh, and the devil makes the world more worldly, the flesh more fleshly, and the devil more devilish by his transgressions. The wildwood is the worse for the wanderer.

F. W. Boreham in *In Pastures Green*

Come, Ye Sinners, Poor and Needy

Come, ye sinners, poor and needy,
Weak and wounded, sick and sore.
Jesus ready stands to save you,
Full of pity, love and power.

Let not conscience make you linger,
Nor of fitness fondly dream;
All the fitness He requireth,
Is to feel your need of Him.

Rev. Joseph Hart

Wallowing in Worry

Being preoccupied with problems precludes resting on the promises.

Much has been written and said about the Prodigal Son. What about the parents—awaking every morning, not from a nightmare, but to one?

I have seen them at times—bravely facing other parents who, like them, had done everything right, and whose children had chosen to follow Christ, while theirs had rejected the Truth and gone.

How, I wonder, did Monica, the mother of Augustine, feel among her friends during those years when her brilliant young son, a leader of the heretical "Manichees," lived in open defiance of God and the Church? (See *Augustine* by Louis Bertrand.)

They Felt Good Eyes upon Them

They felt good eyes upon them
and shrank within—undone;
good parents had good children
and they—a wandering one.

The good folk never meant
to act smug or condemn,
but having prodigals
just "wasn't done" with them.

Remind them gently, Lord,
how You
have trouble with Your children,
too.

Joe Came Home Tonight

Joe came home tonight.
He'd been gone now
quite awhile—
and missed.
Funny how
his absence was felt
more than Charlie's
hanging
'round.
His dad
stayed near that window
day and night,
looking—
listening
for a call that never came.
Joe never missed his dad
like that.
He was too busy
having fun—then pigs—
his own troubles—
himself.
And all the time
his dad
was missing Joe.
Then tonight Joe came
home.

First we knew
the Old Man shouted,
banged the door
and took off down the road.
We saw them meet.
A proud old man
and a bum.
I couldn't believe
Joe could get that dirty
and his dad be so glad
to get him back.
Charlie?
You know Charlie—
faithful but complaining.
Well
he was faithful
to his complaining
tonight.

The rest of us?
Boy! It's great.

P.S. I hope Joe didn't get
a round-trip ticket.

P.P.S. He did.
Where are you, Joe?

A Bit of Broken Wreckage

Another loved prodigal was a spunky little cockney beatnik in London.

Her turning to the Lord was with the faith of a little child.

But her tragic background—drugs and the only profession she knew—were too much. Before I knew it, she was back in the far country.

She has her own child now. So she quit drugs.

"No wai," she said in her Cockney accent, "am I gonna let me child grow up wif drugs. No wai."

I have kept her letters—praying.

When last in London, I got in touch, and we met for pizza. The prodigal is content so far in the far country.

All we can do is pray.

Perhaps She Will Land upon That Shore

Perhaps
she will land
upon That Shore,
not in full sail
but rather,
a bit of broken wreckage
for Him
to gather.

Perhaps
He walks Those shores
seeking such,
who have believed
a little,
suffered much
and so,
been washed Ashore.

Perhaps
of all the souls redeemed
they most
adore.

London, 1972

The Husks Have Greater Zest

Here come I to my own again,
Fed, forgiven, and known again,
Claimed by bone of my bone again,
And sib to flesh of my flesh!

The fatted calf is dressed for me,
But the husks have greater zest for me;
I think my pigs will be best for me,
So I'm off to the styes afresh!

Rudyard Kipling

God and the Stubborn Will

And how does God deal with the stubborn will? Especially when that will is the object of loving, concerned, even desperate prayer?

I found encouragement in *Matthew Henry's Commentary* on Proverbs 21:1. The verse reads: "The king's heart is in the hand of the LORD, as the rivers of water: [H]e turneth it whithersoever [H]e will."

Writes Henry: "God can change men's minds, can turn them from that which they seemed most intent upon, as the husbandman, by canals and gutters, turns the water through his grounds, which does not alter the nature of the water, not put any force upon it, any more than God's providence does upon the native freedom of man's will, but directs the course of it to serve His own purpose."

Nudging the Prodigal Home

God has His own ways of nudging the prodigal home. The men's glee club sang a popular song during my college days (usually reserved for an encore):

> If a nest of wild hornets
> were left in the room,
> And the creatures
> allowed to go free,
> They would not compel
> you to go 'gainst your will
> They'd just make you
> willing to flee.

And there is hope in thine end, saith the Lord, that thy children shall come again to their own border.

Jeremiah 31:17

If I Could Stand Aside

> If I could stand aside
> and see
> him walking through
> Those Splendor'd Gates
> thrown wide,
> instead of me—
> If I could yield my place
> to this, my boy,
> the tears upon my upturned face
> would be
> of joy!

"Thine, O LORD, is the greatness, and the power, and the glory, and the victory, and the majesty: for all that is in the heaven and in the earth is [T]hine; [T]hine is the kingdom, O LORD, and, [T]hou art exalted as head above all.

"Both riches and honor come of [T]hee, and [T]hou reignest over all; and in [T]hine hand is power and might; and in [T]hine hand it is to make great, and to give strength unto all.

"Now therefore, our God, we thank [T]hee, and praise [T]hy glorious name."

David in 1 Chronicles 29:11–13

Can You Trust Me, Child?

Can you trust Me, child?
Not only for ultimate eternity,
    of which you know next to nothing,
    and are not tempted to meddle—
But for the span of your life
    between the Now and Then,
    where you envision decline
        and separations
        and failures, impairments
        pain, bereavements,
        disappointments—
Do you find Me qualified
    to be Lord of your last days?
Oh—yes, Lord!
    YES, Lord!
    Yes and amen!

Can you trust Me, child?
Not only to synchronize the
    unthinkable intricacies of creation—
But to work together for good
    the gravities and tugs
    within your little orbit,
    where your heart is pulled
        by needs and lacks
        you wish, but are destitute,
        to fill—
Do you find My resources adequate
    to feed both the sparrows and you?
Oh—yes, Lord!
    YES, Lord!
    Yes and amen!

Can you trust Me, child
Not only for the oversight
    of nations
    and creations not of this world—
But for those beloved ones
    I committed to you
    and you committed to Me—
Do you believe Me trustworthy
    to perform the good work
    begun in them
until the Day of Jesus Christ?
Oh—yes, Lord!
    YES, Lord!
    Yes and amen!

                    Ann Blochir
                    December 3, 1982

Acknowledgments

I am so grateful for the encouragement and help from Stephen Griffith, who shared my feeling that this book of encouragement for those who love prodigals seems needed, who appreciated the rich contents of old books as I do, and whose advice in putting together the material was invaluable.

And a warm thanks to Evelyn Freeland, who was willing to type whenever needed—frequently beyond the call of duty. And also, I thank my eldest child, Gigi, who has helped with this revision.

Bill Deckard was a great help in reading through the material of the prodigals.

For each whose quotes or poems have encouraged or strengthened, thank you.

To all of these, my warm and grateful thanks.

Notes

Chapter 1

1. Harold C. Gardiner in *The Confessions of St. Augustine*, by Aurelius Augustine, translated by Edward B. Pusey (New York: Pocket Books, 1951), ix.

2. Aurelius Augustine, "The Confessions of St. Augustine," translated by Edward B. Pusey in *Harvard Classic*, vol. 7 (New York: P.F. Collier & Sons Corporation, 1963).

3. Ibid.

4. Ibid., 22.

5. Ibid., 43.

6. Ibid., 42.

7. Ibid., 71.

8. Ibid., 135–36.

9. Malcolm Muggeridge, *A Third Testament* (Boston: Little, Brown, 1976), 29.

Chapter 2

1. John Newton, "An Authentic Narrative," Letter 2, *Newton's Works* (Edinburgh, 1849), 3.

2. Ibid., 4.

3. Ibid.

4. Ibid., Letter 7, 16

5. Ibid.

6. Ibid., 18.

7. Ibid., 16.

8. "Olney Hymns," Book 1, 1 Chronicles #47, 538. Original title is "Faith's Review and Expectation."

9. Bernard Martin, *An Ancient Mariner: A Biography of John Newton* (Dumfries, Virginia: Wyvern Books, 1960), 234.

10. William Jay, *William Jay: An Autobiography* (Banner of Truth edition, 1974), 271.

Chapter 5

1. Schofield Bible, notes to Job 42.

STEPS TO PEACE WITH GOD

1.   RECOGNIZE GOD'S PLAN—PEACE AND LIFE

The message you have read in this book stresses
that God loves you and wants you to
experience His peace and life.

The BIBLE says . . . *"For God loved the
world so much that He gave His only Son,
so that everyone who believes in Him may
not die but have eternal life." John 3:16*

2.   REALIZE OUR PROBLEM—SEPARATION

People choose to disobey God and go
their own way. This results in separation
from God.

The BIBLE says . . . *"Everyone has sinned
and is far away from God's saving
presence." Romans 3:23*

3.   RESPOND TO GOD'S REMEDY—CROSS OF CHRIST

God sent His Son to bridge the gap. Christ
did this by paying the penalty of our sins
when He died on the cross and rose from
the grave.

The BIBLE says . . . *"But God has shown
us how much He loves us—it was while we
were still sinners that Christ died for us!"
Romans 5:8*

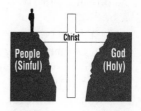

4.   RECEIVE GOD'S SON—LORD AND SAVIOR

You cross the bridge into God's family
when you ask Christ to come into your life.

The BIBLE says . . . *"Some, however, did
receive Him and believed in Him; so He
gave them the right to become God's
children." John 1:12*

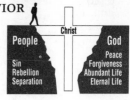

THE INVITATION IS TO:
REPENT (turn from your sins) and by faith RECEIVE Jesus Christ into
your heart and life and follow Him in obedience as your Lord and
Savior.

PRAYER OF COMMITMENT
"Lord Jesus, I know I am a sinner. I believe You died for my sins. Right
now, I turn from my sins and open the door of my heart and life. I
receive You as my personal Lord and Savior. Thank You for saving me
now. Amen."

If you want further help in the decision you have made, write to:
Billy Graham Evangelistic Association
1 Billy Graham Parkway, Charlotte, NC 28201-0001

If you are committing your life to Christ, please let us know! We would like to send you Bible study materials and a complimentary six-month subscription to *Decision* magazine to help you grow in your faith.

The Billy Graham Evangelistic Association exists to support the evangelistic ministry and calling of Billy Graham to take the message of Christ to all we can by every effective means available to us.

Our desire is to introduce as many as we can to the person of Jesus Christ, so that they might experience His love and forgiveness.

Your prayers are the most important way to support us in this ministry. We are grateful for the dedicated prayer support we receive. We are also grateful for those who support us with contributions.

Giving can be a rewarding experience for you and for us at the Billy Graham Evangelistic Association (BGEA). Your gift gives you the satisfaction of supporting an organization that is actively involved in evangelism. Also, it is encouraging to us because part of our ministry is devoted to helping people like you discover and enjoy the stewardship of giving wisely and effectively.

Billy Graham Evangelistic Association
1 Billy Graham Parkway
Charlotte, North Carolina 28201-0001
www.billygraham.org

Billy Graham Evangelistic
Association of Canada
20 Hopewell Way NE
Calgary, Alberta T3J 5H5
www.billygraham.ca

Toll-free: 1-877-247-2426